.the
MiRACLE
of the
SCARLET
thREAD

THE MIRACLE OF THE SCARLET THREAD

EXPANDED EDITION

Revealing the Power of the Blood of Jesus
from Genesis to Revelation

Dr. Richard Booker

DESTINY IMAGE® PUBLISHERS, INC.
P.O. Box 310, Shippensburg, PA 17257-0310
"Promoting Inspired Lives."

This book and all other Destiny Image and Destiny Image Fiction books are available at Christian bookstores and distributors worldwide.

For more information on foreign distributors, call 717-532-3040.
Reach us on the Internet: www.destinyimage.com.

ISBN 13 TP: 978-0-7684-0932-1
ISBN 13 eBook: 978-0-7684-0933-8
HC ISBN: 978-0-7684-1477-6
LP ISBN: 978-0-7684-1476-9

For Worldwide Distribution, Printed in the U.S.A.
6 7 8 / 21 20 19

ACKNOWLEDGMENTS

My love and gratitude to the following:

The reviewers for reading the manuscript and giving helpful comments and needed encouragement.

My wife and covenant partner in life for over 50 years, Peggy, for typing and retyping the manuscript and for being my friend. Many women have done excellently, but she surpasses them all. To her, I lovingly dedicate this writing.

I also want to acknowledge my covenant friend, Randy McLemore, who went to be with the Lord on June 29, 2002. Randy loved this book, gave away many copies and helped spread its message. He is greatly missed by all who knew him and loved him. At Randy's funeral, his pallbearers wore a scarlet thread in their coat lapel as a witness to the impact this book had on their lives. They all made it a point to show it to me and explained why they were wearing it. Wow!

CONTENTS

MY ENCOUNTER WITH GOD

The Story of The Miracle of the Scarlet Thread

Wow! This printing is celebrating 35 years of *The Miracle of the Scarlet Thread* being in print. As you will learn in this preliminary to reading the book, this is truly a miracle. I want to thank my dear friends at Destiny Image Publishers for working with me to issue this anniversary edition of the book.

As a special honor to the Lord for His faithfulness, I have added my personal testimony describing my encounter with God and how this story of the blood of the everlasting covenant became a book. I hope you will be blessed reading how an extraordinary God can change the life of an ordinary person

I have also added two powerful chapters on The Threshold Covenant and The Salt Covenant. Writing these chapters was so exciting and uplifting. I couldn't stop saying, "Wow, Lord, You are awesome." I pray you will experience the same revelation and joy I did when you read them.

Over the years people have asked for a study guide for *The Miracle of the Scarlet Thread.* I am happy to let you know that I have written a separate study guide for individual and/or group use. It is an easy-to-use guide that will take you deeper into this powerful, life-changing story. If you want more, the study guide will help the revelation of this teaching become alive in you. If you are leading a study or reading and studying on your own, I hope you will get a copy and use it along with your study of this book. *You may order the study guide directly from my online store at www.rbooker.com.*

The Revelation of the Blood

I was teaching from *The Miracle of the Scarlet Thread* at a church in Wisconsin when a lady came up to me to tell me her testimony. She told me that she had been asking the Lord for a revelation of the power of His blood. Here is how He answered her prayer.

Shortly after her prayer, she needed surgery. During the surgery the machine she was connected to begin to malfunction. Instead of pumping her blood into her body, it was pumping her blood out of her body. She explained that as the life-giving blood was leaving her body she could feel herself getting weaker and weaker.

She was near death when the doctor realized what was happening and adjusted the machine to work correctly. As her blood was being pumped back into her body, she felt her life coming back and she became stronger with every drop of life-giving blood once again flowing in her body. The Lord then revealed to her that she just experienced the power of His blood.

The Bible reminds us that the life of the flesh is in the blood (Leviticus 17:11). We cannot live without life-giving blood flowing through our body. While human blood is corrupted, the blood of Jesus is pure and has the life of God in it, as John said, "The Word became flesh and dwelt among us" (John 1:14).

God's people are His body on the earth. His Spirit lives in those who are in blood covenant with Him. Spiritually speaking, the Spirit of God gives us a blood transfusion replacing our corrupt, human life-blood with the divine life-blood of Jesus. He is in us and we are in Him. However, if we pump His blood out of us, we will become spiritually weak and spiritually dead.

We all know that the corporate church of Jesus in the West is weak, anemic, and sickly. Many ministers have pumped His blood out of their sermons and given us a transfusion of entertainment—feel-good and self-help sermons that have no power in them. As a result, much of the organized church in the West is near death.

The only thing that will revive the people of God is to spiritually pump the blood of Jesus back into our lives. A transfusion and revelation of His blood will empower us to godly living that will change our lives and the lives of those around us. It is the only thing that will save the Western church and Western civilization from certain spiritual death.

In *The Miracle of the Scarlet Thread* I explain how this happened in my life. I pray the Lord of heaven will use this book to spiritually "pump the blood of Jesus" into your life so that you can walk in the power of His life-giving blood. As this book is a blessing to you, please share it with family, friends and others who may also need this revelation and experience in their journey through life.

My Personal Testimony

It was 1974 that I had an encounter with God and revelation of the blood of Jesus that changed my life forever. I don't know why God prepared and chose me for a divine assignment. I consider myself to be a normal, everyday American person living a normal, everyday American person's life. I don't think of myself to be anyone special. I had no idea that I was born for a purpose or that God had a plan for my life. Does that sound like you? Do you know why you were born or God's plan for your life?

Today is my birthday. Just as I finished writing the above sentence, someone gave me a birthday card that I opened and read. It says, "You were made by a loving God for His special purpose. May today be a celebration of His wonderful plan for you." Now you may think this is just a coincidence, but after walking with God for over forty years I prefer to think that birthday card was really from Him.

I was busy living my life and doing things that American people do. I certainly never had a thought that I would one day leave my successful career to teach the Bible and write Christian books and have no known source of income. I was simply a businessman who started looking for God.

The Bible even talks about the unforeseen plans God has for us. The apostle Paul certainly had a divine surprise in his own life. Writing from firsthand experience, he said, "...Eye has not seen, nor ear heard, nor have entered into the heart of man the things which God has prepared for those who love Him. But God has revealed them to us through His Spirit. For the Spirit searches all things, yes, the deep things of God" (1 Corinthians 2:9-10).

Most people are searching for God but in all the wrong places. They don't really know they are looking for Him. They may have many accomplishments, but they know something is missing in their life. It is not the X factor that is missing but the God factor.

Now here's some good news—if you are truly and sincerely looking for God you will eventually find Him. This is a promise from God as we read in Jeremiah, "And you will seek Me and find Me, when you search for Me with all your heart" (Jeremiah 29:13). Now God doesn't reveal Himself to the casual inquirer. But if you are desperate for Him and are willing to do what He tells you, He will manifest Himself to you.

The Emmaus Road and Leviticus

God manifested Himself to me when I started reading the Bible. I started at Leviticus. I know that is probably not your favorite book in the Bible. It is probably your least favorite. It is my favorite because that is where I met God. I had an Emmaus Road experience while studying the book of Leviticus. What do I mean by an "Emmaus Road experience"?

You recall that after Jesus was resurrected, He appeared to two of His disciples who were walking on the road to the village of Emmaus. They thought that Jesus was the Messiah but lost all hope when He was crucified. They did not know He was raised from the dead. Naturally when He appeared to them, they did not recognize Him. He was the last person they thought they would ever see again—alive!

But then Jesus revealed to them how the Old Testament (Hebrew Bible) was a picture of Himself. Luke explains, "Then their eyes were open and they knew Him; and He vanished from their sight. And they said to one another, 'Did not our heart burn with us while He talked with us on the road, and while He opened the Scriptures to us?'" (Luke 24:31-32). Luke goes on to say that these two disciples began to share what the Lord taught them (Luke 24:35).

In God's predetermined plan for my life, He let me be a third disciple on that road to Emmaus. In other words, God let me in on the teaching. He let me hear what Jesus said to them. But it happened while I was studying Leviticus. It happened so fast I can only explain it as a "heaven second." It was an instant bright picture flash like the flash of a camera.

Using computer talk, God instantly downloaded into my spirit the whole story of the Bible. I saw in a visual revelation that the Hebrew Bible (Old Testament) was a picture of Jesus and how all the pieces, books of the Bible, fit together. The Lord opened my spiritual eyes to see by revelation what I could not see by study alone.

An Encounter with the Almighty

It is very difficult to explain heavenly encounters in earthly terms. Human words fail us. All I can say is that the revelation of God's Word burned in my heart. It was not just knowledge or information; it was revelation and God's revealed Word has God's life in it. The living words of the Living God leaped off the pages of the Bible and came alive in me with His life manifesting Himself in me, through me, and out of me. In other words, I had a spiritual transfusion of the blood of Jesus.

It is this revelation that has been burning in my soul for over forty years. No matter what I may be experiencing in my life, good or bad, joy or sadness, happiness or disappointment, this revelation has empowered me and motivated me to stay the course, run the race, and fight the good fight of faith. And like those two disciples on the Emmaus road, the zeal of God has driven me to share what the Lord taught me.

That burning of the Spirit was not just in my soul. It was also in my body. Before this experience, I knew absolutely nothing about the supernatural and was even told by religious leaders that God no longer did miracles. However, I discovered that when you encounter the Almighty, you can expect to have unusual supernatural manifestations. If you think about it, when the all-powerful God manifests Himself to a human being, you will have "out-of-this-world" experiences. Heaven comes down and glory fills your soul. I am not talking about religion or even "getting saved" but an encounter with the Creator of the universe.

Everyone in the Bible who had an encounter with the Living God was completely undone. When God shows up, everything changes. Your world is turned upside down. Nothing will ever again be the same. The meaning and purpose and focus of your life are set forever. For those who don't believe I can only say that a person who has had an encounter with God is never at the mercy of someone who only has a doctrine or argument about God.

The power of God's revealed Word burst forth out of my spirit into my soul and was being manifested through my body with fire sensations. There were times when my hands were so hot I literally thought I was on fire. I tried to cool my hands by washing them in cold water. This did nothing because the fire was coming from within. I knew that if anyone came near me the holy fire of God's Spirit would touch them in a very tangible way. While this is not a normal experience it is certainly biblical. John the Baptist said that Jesus would baptize us with the Holy Spirit and with fire (see Matthew 3:11).

The Bible speaks about the weight of the glory of God (see 2 Corinthians 4:17). What does this mean? It means that the finite creature cannot take too much revelation and manifestation of the infinite Creator. Perhaps you recall when God showed up at Mount Sinai His presence was too much for the people. They asked Moses to speak with God for them (see Exodus 20:19).

When I had my encounter with God, the weight of His glory was so heavy there were a few times when I could neither walk nor stand. I crawled on the floor in my house trying to get to the couch. All I could do was to slowly pull myself along on my elbows and knees just to go a few feet. When I finally got to the couch, it took all of my strength to roll myself up on the couch. All I could do was lay there motionless until the weight of His glory lifted. I could not move. These are moments you never forget.

You see, the infinite Creator can only reveal a little of Himself to finite humans. If He manifests too much of Himself, we would die. I thought I would die and literally hid under my desk and begged God not to show me anything further. I thought I would explode. Really, this is the way it happened. The power of His living Word in me was more than my fragile human flesh could handle.

Forsaking All to Follow His Call

Thank God He knows what we can take. God knew I needed such a powerful manifestation of His presence to make such a drastic change in my life. I am forever grateful that He was also revealing Himself to my wife, Peggy, who had the faith and trust in God to accept His calling in our lives, as this would mean leaving my career with no money and no visible means of support.

I was 32 years of age when I had this encounter that would forever change my life. At the time I was at the peak of my career path enjoying my position as Corporate Director of Management Information Systems Training and Standards at a large oil company in Houston, Texas. But when one meets the Living God in such a powerful way, everything you used to glory in no longer matters. I instantly lost all interest in my career and job. I stopped watching football games, turned off the television, and every other distraction fell by the wayside. All I wanted to do was to "eat the book." I felt I could not live unless I could spend every waking minute in the presence of God studying His holy Word.

With such a hot fire of God burning in my heart, I could no longer function at my job. Peggy and I came to understand that God was calling me to a life of study and ministry. But what do we do? That work doesn't pay too well. If I left my job we had no stocks to sell, no bonds to cash, no severance pay or retirement, not even any savings, no supporters, and no known source of money to pay the bills. While there is a difference between faith and presumption, the Lord gave us the faith to trust Him to take care of us as we followed His call and plan for our lives.

In those days there was no one to mentor us or help us understand the dramatic change in our lives. Of course people didn't understand how I could just quit my job with no source of income. We didn't understand it either, but it really didn't matter if we understood it or not. The zeal of God was consuming us and that was all that mattered. As we say, it was sink or swim. The Lord was gracious and encouraged us with the following Scripture, "But seek first the kingdom of God and His righteousness, and all these things shall be added to you" (Matthew 6:33).

We came to believe that God wanted me to teach the Bible and write Christian books beginning with sharing my experience and revelation of the blood covenant. In those days, few Christians understood the ministry gift of "teacher." We spent a lot of time trying to explain my calling. As we were leaving everything we knew and were familiar with, we needed God to confirm this for us. He did so in several ways, one of which was so clear we knew we were hearing from Him. Here is what happened.

I picked up a book by Frances Roberts entitled *On the Highroad of Surrender* (King's Farspan, Inc., 1973). As I looked at the Table of Contents, my eyes seemed to be directed by an unseen hand to a specific inspirational topic. It was called "My Words Cannot Wait." I turned to page 38 and read the following words.

"The hour is late, and the time for ministering is limited. Delay not, but hasten to finish the work. I have other work for you, and it only waits the completion of the present task. Do that which is nearest at hand. I shall open a way for its fulfillment, so you need not hold back, wondering how the provisions will be supplied. Lacked you ever in the present? Have you not acted in each case with faith in Me as your only hope? Yes, child, I say to you, walk on. There are no limits to the promises of God.

"My words cannot wait; but you have held them as though you thought the future would wait. Up! Delay no more. Obey Me, and do so quickly. There is a door open that may soon be shut. There are hearts ready that will be turned in discouragement to error but for your words. Send forth the message and trust Me with its end. I hold all things in My power, and I shall direct its goings. Do not analyze the situation, nor seek to protect yourself from misunderstanding nor My words from rejection.

"Lo, the Spirit accompanies the word, and you may know and be confident that My Spirit anointing the page will bring light and revelation and the confession that God has truly spoken. Yield and labor. I will add the blessing and the reward. I have called you by name. I have given you My words, and I will not have them set aside either by you or by others. Renew your faith. Look directly to Me. I will empower and I will make all things possible as you move in obedience."

Wow! What an answer from God. With this confirmation, I wrote *The Miracle of the Scarlet Thread* and many other books that God has used just as He said to bring light and revelation and encouragement to many. While it has never been easy and there have been many obstacles, God has been faithful to His word. He is a faithful, covenant-keeping God.

At the time of this writing, Peggy and I have been married for 50 years and been in the ministry for over 40 years. I could not have accomplished God's will for my life without Peggy. There are many great women in the world, but to me she is the greatest of them all. Our lives together began when we met on a blind date on New Year's Eve in 1964. Even our names are prophetic. My name is Booker and I write books. Peggy's maiden name is Harper and she plays the harp (autoharp).

We still the live the same life of faith as in those early days trusting God to provide for our needs. Even though we started with no money and still live from day to day with no known source of income, we have been blessed to give hundreds of thousands of dollars to help others and to advance the Kingdom of God on the earth.

The Miracle of This Book

There are so many stories about the faithfulness of God I wish I could share with you. *The Miracle of the Scarlet Thread* has its own history. Spiritual opposition to the revelation of the power of

His blood has tried to destroy this book. For example, publishing companies didn't want to publish a book by an unknown author. The simple act of opening the mail became a dramatic "holding our breath" experience. We had stacks of rejection letters and pre-printed rejection postcards. While this was discouraging, the zeal of God motivated us not to give up in our efforts to get the book into print. This was not something we could do or wanted to do; it was something we had to do.

When finally published, at our own expense, *The Miracle of the Scarlet Thread* went through the hands of various publishers. Several of them went out of business, which made the book unavailable. At one time in its history, the book was locked up in a dusty warehouse and inaccessible. Another time the printing plates for the book were destroyed. Another time five thousand copies were misprinted and had to be destroyed. Are you getting what is happening? However you view this, spiritual forces do not want people to read this book. They fear the power of the blood of Jesus.

We are forever grateful how God has used this book to dramatically impact the lives of thousands of people. As one friend said, "This book is a game changer." The fact that it is still in print after 35 years is a miracle in itself. But God is faithful. Heaven and earth will pass away, but God's Word abides forever. We are thankful that God has let us live long enough to see the fruit of this book. We have heard from so many people around the world. If this book is a blessing to your life, we would love to hear from you.

I wanted to share this background so you can know something of the author and the story of *The Miracle of the Scarlet Thread*. What I have written is not just information. It came out of the revelation and manifestation of God Himself calling me to share with you what He showed me on that Emmaus Road experience. I hope that you will not only come to better know the story of the Bible but, more importantly, the One who wrote it, the author, God Himself.

After all these years, now decades, I still consider myself to be an ordinary person, but I have encountered an extraordinary God and so can you. I pray that as you read and study *The Miracle of the Scarlet Thread*, you too will have an encounter with the Living God. May He reveal more of Himself to you, and may His words come alive in you with fire and power. May they bring light and revelation and the confession that God truly has spoken to your heart. May you have a fresh transfusion of the pure and holy, life-giving blood of Jesus.

PREFACE

Have you ever sat down to read the Bible, hoping it would all make sense to you, but it didn't make sense? You probably started at Genesis expecting any loose ends to knit together as you weaved your way through.

But a frustrating thing happened on your way to Revelation. As you threaded through chapter after chapter, you noticed the loose ends didn't knit together. In fact, they got more tangled... tangled with rituals, events, customs and strange happenings that didn't seem to fit into any pattern.

Instead of finding a finished garment beautifully interwoven with divine truth into a God given pattern, loose ends seem to run in all directions. There didn't seem to be any order to what you were reading. So, in despair, you gave up.

Well, that was me. As a Christian, I had read the Bible, but I never could quite put it all together. What particularly puzzled me was how the Hebrew Bible (what Christians call the Old Testament) and the New Testament were related, if at all. The Bible seemed to be two different books that somehow got stuck under one cover. I never really said that, but in the back of my mind I wondered about it.

From now on when I refer to the Hebrew Bible I will use the phrase "Old Testament" simply because that is the name most people use when referring to the first part of the Bible. This is not to imply that the Hebrew Bible is outdated and no longer relevant or that it has been replaced by the New. It is old only in the sense that it was written chronologically before the "Newer Testament." In fact, the teachings in the New Testament are simply a continuation of the teachings in the First Testament as they find their goal in Jesus.

Little did I know that both Testaments were telling the same story; that God did have an order to His book. He did have a divine pattern.

After God filled me with His Holy Spirit, He began to reveal His pattern to me. He showed me that from Genesis to Revelation, the Bible tells one story. The story is that God has entered into a blood covenant with Himself for mankind through Jesus of Nazareth, the Son of God, Messiah of the Jews, and Savior of the Gentiles. And all who will, may enter into the covenant with Him.

The blood covenant is the "scarlet thread" that runs through the entire Bible. All other teachings are woven into it. Once you understand the blood covenant, your biblical loose ends will come together. You will see God's order. You will see God's heavenly pattern.

That's why I have written this book...to help you see the beautiful "Garment of Salvation" God has woven in His Holy Word. He wants you to put it on and wear it. If you do, it will change your life forever as it did mine. May the One True God of Abraham, Isaac, and Jacob bless you as you discover His incredible covenant fully and completely revealed to us through Jesus.

Chapter 1

INTRODUCTION TO A DUSTY OLD BOOK

That Dusty Old Book

For many years after becoming a Christian, I tried to find life in the words of the Bible. I really did believe the Bible was God's inspired word, but it never came alive in my spirit. When I would read the Bible, all the stories ran together. It was like putting together a stamp book. If you've ever done that, you know how dry your mouth is after licking all those stamps. Well that's the way the Bible left me in my soul, dry and thirsty. Of course, that's not the way it was supposed to be, but that's the way it was.

Perhaps this describes your experience with the Bible. If so, that is all going to change. God's holy Word is about to leap off the pages into your heart. Your life is never going to be the same.

It's a Mystery to Me

I was blessed with a good education and had been successful in my profession as a computer consultant. Because of my background, order and logic were important to me. This is what I kept looking for in the Bible but somehow it escaped me.

The biggest mystery of all was how the Old Testament and the New Testament were related. I had taken to heart God's salvation message through Jesus in the New Testament. But I could see very little, if any, practical spiritual value in the Old Testament. I recognized it as a historical collection of Jewish writings but couldn't see how it had anything to do with the carpenter from Nazareth in the New Testament. I always thought that the Old Testament was written for Jews and the New Testament was written for Christians. I thought they were different books for different people. Wow, was I ever wrong!

Something else puzzled me even more. *How could this dusty Old Testament, written by men thousands of years ago, in an oriental, agricultural setting have anything to say to a modern, sophisticated, westernized technologically oriented, freeway driving, city slicker?* That was me. I could program a computer, interpret the financial pages of Wall Street, and quote the buzzwords of the latest management fads, but I couldn't understand the Bible.

Many times I picked up the Bible and began reading, determined to make sense out of it. But my good intentions didn't last very long. Soon I found myself putting the Bible back on the shelf. There it took its place among the other books, gathering dust and collecting cobwebs. I didn't understand that the Bible is a spiritual book that can only be understood as the Spirit of God reveals it to hungry hearts,

An Idol That Couldn't Help

Then in 1974, God revealed to me the main reason why I couldn't understand the Bible. *He showed me that I had an idol in my life.* That idol was my career. It was more important to me than God.

Because I pursued my career with great zeal, it brought me material comforts and the praise of men. Yet, it was a costly idol. What it cost me was the ability to receive the fresh breath of life from God Almighty flowing in my spirit. I've since learned that this is a tradeoff no human being can afford to make; because only God can satisfy the longings and cries of a human heart. Only God can bring peace to a restless soul. Only God can fill that void within each of us.

My career and the trappings that went with it were not meeting these needs in my life. *Yet it was a barrier keeping me from knowing the fullness of God.* I was experiencing what I call the "Christian credibility gap." God promises to personally reveal His grace and glory to all who will come to Him through Jesus. Well, I had come to Him through Jesus but I was not experiencing His grace and glory.

You see, God could not reveal Himself to me through the Bible, because I would not draw near to Him. But finally, in the midst of worldly success, I knew I would never really be fulfilled until I sought God with my whole heart and completely gave my life to Him.

God Feeds the Hungry

Once again I picked up the Bible. But this time I had more than just a casual interest. This time I was hungry for God.

More than anything in the world, I wanted to know the power of His resurrection life. I wanted to be strengthened by His Spirit in my inner self. I wanted to receive wisdom and revelation knowledge of God. I wanted to know the breadth, length, height, and depth of God's love. I wanted to be filled with His fullness and experience communion with my Creator.

God honored that desire of my heart and filled me with His Spirit. With this fresh commitment, energy, and motivation, I made a renewed effort to understand the Bible. After I dusted off the cobwebs, God directed me to read the book of Leviticus from the Old Testament. Now to me, the book of Leviticus had always been the driest of all the books in the Bible. Why would God have me read *that* book? Why wouldn't He have me read something relevant and exciting, like the Gospel of John?

A Heavenly Portrait

It didn't take long for me to find out. With the Holy Spirit now teaching me, I began to see God's order in the Bible. I began to see the picture that God was painting from Genesis to Revelation. Once I saw the big picture, the individual pieces began to come together and make sense. And with very little effort on my part.

The painting that God showed me in the Old Testament was a startling discovery. It was a picture of Jesus. At first I couldn't believe what I was seeing. It was almost too good to be true. But the more I studied the Old Testament, the clearer the picture became. *God was showing me that He gave the entire Old Testament as a picture of His salvation message in Jesus of Nazareth.* The picture was in shadow form represented by what had seemed to be meaningless rituals, customs, places, names, and unrelated happenings. But they were all individual pieces of the same picture. The picture came into focus as God lifted the veil off my spiritual eyes. I could see Jesus all through the Old Testament.

God showed me this was the whole reason why He gave us the Old Testament. It was to point us to Jesus who was God in the flesh coming to reconcile His creation to Himself. Many people say that Jesus never claimed to be God. This is simply not true. Every time Jesus opened His mouth, He claimed to be God. Now He never said the words "I am God." That would have meant nothing to those listening. Anybody could come along and say that. And many did. *But Jesus made His claims within the framework that the people were anticipating and would understand.* That framework was the Old Testament shadow that would direct people to Him as the light of the world.

Some say that it is blasphemous to believe that God became a man. But God's eternal covenant plan required Him to become one of us in order to redeem us. God became our "near-kinsman" in the person of Jesus of Nazareth. This is the story of the Bible from Genesis to Revelation and the story of this book.

You see, God had planned, that in His own appointed time, He would prepare for Himself a body just like ours and become one of us. Since He is God, He naturally knew everything He would do when He became one of us. He knew where He would be born. He knew by what name He would be called. He knew everything about the details of His life. He even knew how he would die. Therefore, He painted this shadow of Himself in the Old Testament so that everybody would recognize Him when He arrived on the scene. This is how the entire Old Testament points to Jesus. *It is a picture of a person.*

Isn't this what we would do if we were going to meet someone who had never seen us before? Why, we would describe ourselves in great detail and even decide beforehand where we would meet. That way the person looking for our coming would recognize us when we show up.

A Word From Jesus

Jesus confirmed that the entire Old Testament was simply a portrait of Himself. As a result, the only written word from God that man needed up to the time of Jesus was the Old Testament. When Jesus and the New Testament writers referred to the "Scriptures" or "Scripture", they were speaking of the Old Testament. It had been translated from Hebrew to Greek in about 250 B.C. It is the identical Old Testament that is in the present day Protestant Bible. Jesus and the New Testament writers acknowledged it as the inspired Word of God. Jesus said that it all pointed to Him.

One day when Jesus was talking to some of the Jewish leaders, He made this statement, "You search the Scriptures, for you believe they give you eternal life. And the Scriptures point to me! Yet you won't come to me so that I can give you this life eternal" (John 5:39-40 TLB).

What Jesus said to those Jewish leaders described my situation. I had searched the Scriptures looking for life in God's Word. But it didn't come alive to me because I had not completely surrendered to Jesus as Lord of my life. Therefore, He couldn't reveal Himself to me. When I finally wanted Him more than anything else, the Bible came alive. I found it to be more than pretty paper and print with a few words printed in red. It was God-breathed and He was breathing it into my spirit through the Holy Spirit. He was writing it on my heart. God's word became flesh in me, an ordinary human being.

Well, some of these Jewish leaders wouldn't believe Jesus because they loved the praise of men more than the praise of God. Their pride and tradition has become a barrier to them just like my career had been a barrier to me.

Jesus then told them,

> *"Yet it is not I who will accuse you of this to the Father—Moses will! Moses, on whose laws you set your hopes of heaven. For you have refused to believe Moses. He wrote about me, but you refuse to believe him, so you refuse to believe in me. And since you don't believe what he wrote, no wonder you don't believe me either"* (John 5:45-46 TLB).

A lot of people today seek to discredit Moses' authorship of the first five books of the Bible. They also disclaim the literalness of these writings. This attack of the Bible goes under the name of the "higher criticism." That sounds very sophisticated, but Jesus didn't think much of man's "higher criticism." *Jesus said that Moses wrote the first five books of the Bible and that Moses was writing about Him.* Therefore, if a person doesn't clearly perceive with "the eyes of their spirit" what God said about Himself through Moses, neither will he or she believe Jesus as He presents Himself as the Messiah and only Savior of the world.

Jesus Comments on Jesus

What did God say about Himself through the Old Testament writers? Once again, Jesus provides the commentary. By the time Jesus came along, the Jewish sages had divided the Old Testament into three divisions. These were the Law of Moses, the Prophets, and the Psalms.

Anytime someone used these references, they were talking about the complete Old Testament.

After Jesus was resurrected, He appeared to His disciples in Jerusalem. "He said to them, 'This is what I told you while I was still with you: Everything must be fulfilled that is written about me in the Law of Moses, the Prophets, and the Psalms'" (Luke 24:44 NIV).

With this statement, *Jesus was again claiming that the writers of the Old Testament, from Genesis to Malachi, were writing about Him.* The disciples must have looked puzzled. So Jesus explained what the Old Testament writers said about Him.

Luke records it for us. He says,

> "'Then He [Jesus] *opened their minds so they could understand the Scriptures. He told them, This is what is written: The Christ* [Messiah] *will suffer and rise from the dead on the third day, and repentance and forgiveness of sins will be preached in his name to all nations, beginning at Jerusalem'"* (Luke 24:45-46 NIV).

Unlocking the Mystery

Jesus opened their minds by telling them the key for understanding the Scriptures. He told His disciples that the Old Testament writers wrote of His crucifixion and resurrection for the forgiveness of sins. *This is how the two testaments are linked together.* They both tell this one story. The Old Testament tells that it is going to happen. The New Testament tells that it *did* happen.

It is the story of God entering into a blood covenant with Himself for mankind through Jesus.

The covenant in the blood of Jesus is the "scarlet thread" that runs through both testaments. This is what Jesus wanted us to know when He said, "Don't misunderstand why I have come—it isn't to cancel the laws of Moses and the warnings of the prophets. No, I came to fulfill them, and to make them all come true" (Matthew 5:17 TLB).

A Book-by-Book Account

Some people find this truth too simple to believe. Jesus anticipated that they might. So, to further confirm it, He appeared to two disciples on the road to Emmaus, a city about seven miles from Jerusalem. They were followers of Jesus and were saddened by His death. At first they didn't recognize Him.

But after walking with them a ways, Jesus said to them,

> "'...You are such foolish, foolish people! You find it so hard to believe all that the prophets wrote in the Scriptures! Wasn't it clearly predicted by the prophets that the Messiah would have to suffer all these things before entering his time of glory?' Then Jesus quoted them passage after passage from the writings of the prophets beginning with the book of Genesis and going right on through the Scriptures, explaining what the passages meant and what they said about Himself" (Luke 24:25-27 TLB).

That must have been some teaching session. Jesus showed them the "scarlet thread" of the covenant in His blood throughout the Old Testament. We, too, can discover this for our own lives when we look through the eyes of the Holy Spirit. St. Augustine expressed this key to understanding the Bible when he wrote, "The New is in the Old contained; the Old is by the New explained."

As I've used this key in studying the Old Testament, Jesus, through the Holy Spirit, has opened my mind to understand the

Scriptures. He has shown me how the Old Testament writers were speaking of Himself in His crucifixion and resurrection for the forgiveness of sins. He has led me to write this book to help others understand the Scriptures through this divine key.

A Preview of What's Ahead

In this introductory chapter, you've seen Jesus claim that the Old Testament is more than just meaningless rituals, customs, and unrelated events. *On the contrary, it is an orderly, progressive, unfolding revelation from God, of the sacred blood covenant God has entered into with mankind through Jesus, our Savior and Lord.*

You have learned the key for understanding the Scriptures is to look for the "scarlet thread" of the covenant as it points to the blood of Jesus. This is what you will be reading in this book. I pray this key will leap off the pages into your heart as you follow the story of the covenant that God has entered into with His creation.

Now since Jesus Himself told us what to look for in the Scriptures, *what you will be reading in this book is not someone's personal opinion or private interpretation of the Scriptures.* For those who want to know the Word of God rather than the word of man, this should be comforting. In this book, the Bible will provide its own commentary.

Chapters 2 through 7 are divided into three major headings: Background, Old Covenant, and New Covenant. The background information provides the necessary historical perspective for understanding the setting of the chapter. It will also help you follow the progressive unfolding of the covenant. The Old Covenant information describes the covenant as God gave it in shadow form. The

New Covenant writing explains how Jesus perfectly fulfilled the Old and how we relate to Him in the New.

In Chapter 2, you will learn *what the blood covenant is* and why it was necessary for God to establish this means for man to approach Him. You'll actually participate in the blood covenant ceremony as two Hebrew males would have done it. Don't panic at this point! Your participation will be on paper only. You won't have to give blood. Then you will study the covenant as it was entered into by David and Jonathan. Afterward, you'll see how Jesus completes the covenant and how you may enter into it through Him.

Chapter 3 tells how *God reconfirmed the covenant through Abraham*. You'll have a ringside seat of the covenant ceremony between God and Abraham. You'll uncover what it was that Abraham believed that caused God to declare him righteous. You'll see why Jesus could say that Abraham saw His day and rejoiced in it (John 8:56). You may be surprised when you find out who is a Jew in God's eyes.

In Chapter 4, you will *stand on Mount Sinai with Moses and receive the Ten Commandments.* But you'll also learn how to build a Tabernacle. As you examine its furnishings, God will lead you through it to Jesus of Nazareth, the real Tabernacle of God that was made without hands. All who know Jesus as the divine/human Tabernacle of God may also become the dwelling place of God in the Spirit.

Chapter 5 follows the covenant as God progressively reveals it through the *innocent substitutionary sacrifice.* You'll find yourself at the Tabernacle making sacrifices before the Lord. There at the altar, God will give you detailed instructions so that each sacrifice will uniquely reveal something to you about the nature of the perfect sacrifice in Jesus. All who have accepted Jesus as their sin sacrifice not only have their sins covered, but they have been taken away to be remembered no more.

Chapter 6 describes the covenant as God revealed it in the *High Priest*. You'll see Him in his garments of glory and beauty and anxiously watch as he intercedes for you on the Day of Atonement. God will focus your eyes toward a future High Priest, the Lord Jesus, who came as the perfect mediator between God and man. In Him, all may be accepted before God and inherit the kingdom prepared from the foundations of the world.

In Chapter 7, you will learn how God revealed the covenant in the *Passover celebration*. From the blood of the lamb over the doorpost in Egypt, God will lead you to the real Lamb who came to take away the sins of the world. That Lamb is Jesus. All who will receive Him as their Passover offering will receive the life of God within them and experience communion with their Creator.

Look for Jesus

Sound exciting? It surely is. It's the most exciting news in the world. An unknown author put it this way:

> I find my Lord in the Bible
> Wherever I chance to look,
> He is the theme of the Bible
> The center and heart of the Book;
> He is the Rose of Sharon,
> He is the Lily fair,
> Wherever I open my Bible
> The Lord of the Book is there.
>
> He, at the Book's beginning,
> Gave to the earth its form,
> He is the Ark of shelter

Bearing the brunt of the storm,
The Burning Bush of the desert,
The budding of Aaron's Rod,
Wherever I look in the Bible
I see the Son of God.

The Ram upon Mt. Moriah,
The Ladder from earth to sky,
The Scarlet Cord in the window,
And the Serpent lifted high,
The Smitten Rock in the desert,
The Shepherd with staff and crook,
The face of my Lord I discover
Wherever I open the Book.
He is the Seed of the Woman,
The Savior Virgin-born;
He is the Son of David,
Whom men rejected with scorn,
His garments of grace and beauty
The stately Aaron deck,
Yet He is a Priest forever,
For He is Melchizedek.

Lord of eternal glory
Whom John, the Apostle, saw;
Light of the Golden City,
Lamb without spot or flaw,
Bridegroom coming at midnight,
For whom the Virgins look.
Wherever I open my Bible,
I find my Lord in the Book.

As you read the pages of this book, I pray that God will powerfully reveal to you His grace and glory. I pray that God's beloved Jewish people will come to know their Messiah, Yeshua (the Hebrew way of saying Jesus), and enter into the New Covenant through His blood atonement. I pray that *Gentiles* will come to know the power of the blood of Jesus to reconcile them to God and bring forgiveness of sins. For *Christians*, I pray they will come to know their Heavenly Father more intimately and receive the *fullest measure* of His Spirit operating in their lives.

Jesus in Every Book of the Bible

Jesus in the Law

- Genesis—The Seed of Woman
- Exodus—The Passover Lamb
- Leviticus—The Perfect Sacrifice
- Numbers—The Lifted-Up One
- Deuteronomy—The Prophet Greater than Moses

Jesus in the Books of History

- Joshua—The Captain of our Salvation
- Judges—The Deliverer
- Ruth—The Near Kinsman
- Samuel—The Judge
- Kings and Chronicles—The King
- Ezra—The Faithful Scribe
- Nehemiah—The Restorer of Our Soul
- Esther—The Advocate

Jesus in the Books of Poetry

- Job—The Ever-Living Redeemer
- Psalms—The New Song

- Proverbs—The Wisdom of God
- Ecclesiastes—The Goal of Life
- Song of Solomon—Lover of Our Soul

Jesus in the Major Prophets

- Isaiah—The Suffering Servant
- Jeremiah—Righteous Branch of David
- Lamentation—The Weeping Prophet
- Ezekiel—The Glory of God
- Daniel—The Smiting Stone & Fourth Man

Jesus in the Minor Prophets

- Hosea—The Forgiving Bridegroom
- Joel—The Giver of the Holy Spirit
- Amos—The Builder of the City of God
- Obadiah—The Savior
- Jonah—The First-Born from the Dead
- Micah—The Ruler of all Ages
- Nahum—The Avenger
- Habakkuk—The God of Our Salvation
- Zephaniah—The One in Our Midst
- Haggai—The Restorer of the Kingdom
- Zechariah—The Priest on the Throne
- Malachi—The Sun of Righteousness with Healing in His wings

Jesus in the Gospels

- Matthew—The King of the Jews

- Mark—The Servant
- Luke—The Son of Man
- John—The Son of God

Jesus in Formation of the Church

- Acts—The Giver of the Holy Spirit

Jesus in Paul's Letters

- Romans—The Justifier of Sinners
- Corinthians—The Giver of Gifts
- Galatians—The Liberator of our Soul
- Ephesians—The Exalted One
- Philippians—Our Joy
- Colossians—The Head of all Things
- Thessalonians—The Hope of Mankind
- Timothy and Titus—Pastor and Shepherd
- Philemon—Our Covenant Friend

Jesus in the General Letters

- Hebrews—The Messenger of the New Covenant
- James—The Great Physician
- Peter—The Cornerstone
- 1, 2, 3 John—Love, Light, and Truth
- Jude—The One Who is Able to Keep Us

Jesus in Revelation

- Revelation—The King of Kings and Lord of Lords

Chapter 2

THE BLOOD COVENANT

Background

Have you ever heard someone say, "I don't believe in God?" I've heard people say that before. I've heard others say that they're not sure if God exists. They question the existence of a God who, in their way of thinking, allows so much sorrow on the face of the earth.

The Bible says that a person who talks this way is a fool (Psalm 53:1). The Bible says this because God has clearly revealed

Himself to all of humanity. God has made the fact of His existence known to us through nature and instinct.

All we have to do to realize there is a God is to open our eyes and look at His creation. Have you ever wondered how the snow knows just when to fall? How the rain knows just when to drop? How the clouds know just when to open up? How the sun knows just when to rise and set? How the moon knows just when to shine? How the tide knows when it's supposed to be high and when it's supposed to be low? How the seasons know just when to change? How is it that all of creation, except man, functions with perfect order and harmony?

Well the answer, of course, is that there is a God in heaven who has created all things. And He is a God of order. His creative order testifies to His existence. King David, the sweet Psalmist of Israel, said it this way, "*The heavens* declare the glory of God; and the firmament sheweth his handiwork" (Psalm 19:1 KJV, emphasis mine).

A thousand years later, another Jew by the name of Paul, said, "Since earliest times men have seen the earth and sky and all God made and have known of his existence and great eternal power. So they will have no excuse (when they stand before God at Judgment Day)" (Romans 1:20 TLB).

Not only do we know that God exists through His handiwork, but we also know of His existence through instinct. We all have a built-in, God-consciousness. No matter how far away we may be from God, we still know that He is around. Our conscience, regardless of how hardened it may be, constantly reminds us that there is a God in heaven who created us in His image. No matter how much we deny Him, we are hard-wired with a God-conscious DNA to believe in a Creator-God.

The Bible puts it this way, "For the truth about God is known to them instinctively; God has put this knowledge in their hearts" (Romans 1:19 TLB). Therefore, the Bible never attempts to prove God's existence. It assumes His existence and simply says that anyone who does otherwise is obviously a fool.

Once we acknowledge the existence of God, our next logical pursuit is to find out about Him. *Who is this God and what is He like?* In other words, we should get to know Him. It seems that most people know "about" God, but they don't "know" Him. The typical attitude seems to be that God is God. He's the Creator. He's the all-mighty, all-knowing, all-powerful one. He's the one who said, "Let there be" and there was. He's the everlasting source of eternal life, and in Him is life.

While man, well, he's man. He's the creation. He's uncertain of the mysteries of life. He's not all-knowing, not all-powerful, and not all-mighty. He's weak and fragile. His body aches. He gets sick. He suffers. He dies. In man is death.

So as man observes the power of God in the wind, rain, fire, earthquakes, floods, tornadoes, hurricanes, the changing seasons, and birth, life, and death, his fallen conscience testifies to a distant Deity who sits looking over him from way up there somewhere in the high and holy place. God is considered an impersonal influence and there is no personal identification with Him.

Perhaps this is your understanding of God. It was mine for a long time. *To me, God was always the stern Judge hiding behind the harsh bar of the Ten Commandments.* I thought He was just waiting for me to get out of line so He could club me with one of His stone tablets. I believed this way because I only knew "about" God; I didn't "know" Him.

However, God tells a different story about Himself. He says that He loves us and wants to bless us. *Do you know that God loves you and wants to bless you?* He does! And to prove that He loves us, He has taken the initiative to enter into an eternal covenant of love with us. This covenant of love is available to all who will enter into it.

When you enter into this covenant, you come to a personal consciousness and awareness of God as your Heavenly Father. And as you get to know Him, you discover that He's not like any earthly father. Love is the expression of the Heavenly Father. He loves us so much that He gave Himself for us. He's not only perfect love, but He is love.

He's not some distant Deity who stands apart and aloof from our trials. Nor does He sit sternly in condemnation over us. There is no condemnation for those who have entered into covenant with Him. On the contrary, because He has identified Himself with us through the birth, life, and death of His Son, He completely understands us. Therefore, He is able to fully and completely enter into all our trials.

Since He made us, He understands our limitations. So, He is sympathetic to our struggles. He remembers that we were born and shaped in iniquity. He knows that our brief journey on earth is but a fleeting moment in which we constantly war against the attacks of the world on our soul.

He knows our hearts because He knows our makeup. He was there before we were formed in our mother's womb. So we can come to Him without pretense, just as we are. He will receive us with compassion, kindness, understanding and affection.

He is merciful and gracious towards us. He is slow to anger. He is good and ready to forgive. He has plenty of mercy. His loving-kindness is always extended to us.

He is righteous in all His ways and holy in all His works. Since He is perfectly righteous, we can trust Him to always do the right thing by us. He will never "set us up."

Because He loves us; He must discipline us. But His discipline is always perfectly just. It is always fair and consistent and for our own good. We can trust Him to move all events for the purpose of sharing His glory with us.

Even though He knows the worst about us, He still loves us. We can always find a warm reception at "Father's" house. We are the constant object of His love and attention. His concern and care for us is never ending. His patience, compassion, mercy, fairness and understanding are always extended to us. Whatever our situation, we can have a calm assurance that He is ours and we are His. As we get to know Him, His perfect love casts out all fear we may have of Him.

Is this the God you know? He can be, because this is who He is. God says to each of us, "... Let not the wise man glory in his wisdom, let not the mighty man glory in his might, let not the rich man glory in his riches; but let him who glories glory in this, that he understands and knows me, that I am the LORD who practice steadfast love, justice, and righteousness in the earth; for in these things I delight, says the Lord" (Jeremiah 9:23-24 RSV).

Whatever your status in life, God wants you to know Him. He wants you to enter into this covenant of love with Him. This is the story of the Bible. It's the story of this book. It's the story of how God loves us so much that He gave His only Son as the sacrifice for our sins. And whoever will enter into covenant with Him shall not perish but have everlasting life. (See John 3:16.)

Covenant Defined

Bible students know that the Bible is divided into two divisions: the Old Testament and the New Testament. The word testament comes from a Latin word, *testamentum*. The more proper name for these two divisions; however, is "covenant." So the Bible is really the story of an Old(er) Covenant and a New(er) Covenant. From now on I'll be using the word covenant rather than testament when referring to the ritual described in the Bible

Now, in the Bible, the word covenant means a binding agreement between two parties. The Hebrew word for covenant is Berith. The Greek word is Diatheke. It actually means to "cut covenant." By definition, it is an agreement to "cut a covenant by the shedding of blood and walking between pieces of flesh." So the two divisions in the Bible are about an Old(er) Blood Covenant and a New(er) Blood Covenant.

A blood covenant between two parties is the closest, the most enduring, the most solemn and the most sacred of all contracts. It absolutely cannot be broken. When you enter into blood covenant with someone, you promise to give them your life, your love, and your protection forever...till death do you part. Marriage is a blood covenant. We don't honor marriage as a blood covenant but God says it is. (see Malachi 2:14; Proverbs 2:17.)

When the bride and groom feed each other the wedding cake, they are saying symbolically, "I'm coming into you and you into me. The two of us are becoming one." This symbolic union is made complete by the physical act of marriage when the groom and bride come together as husband and wife. The blood covenant is consummated when the hymen is broken. You see now why God says pre and extra-marital physical intercourse is a sin.

(see Exodus 20:14; Matthew 5:27; 1 Corinthians 6:18; 10:8; Galatians 5:19.)

The reason we wear the wedding ring on the third finger is because man believed that the third finger had a nerve leading to the heart. And since the heart is the central part of the body that keeps the blood circulating, it became the symbol of life.

We use the word "heart" to represent the total person. It stands for your whole being, your whole nature, your whole life. When you love someone with all your heart, you love them with all your being. When you give your heart to someone, you are giving them your total life. This is the essence and spirit of the blood covenant which God ordains in the Bible and that man has always recognized.

The Hebrew Ritual

The Hebrews had a blood covenant ritual that was similar to the other nations around them. All nations practiced blood covenant because man instinctively sought this relationship. So this practice was not unique to the Hebrews. When studying ancient blood covenant rituals, I realized they all had certain common elements. For ease of understanding, I have organized these common elements into the following nine steps along with a Scripture reference for each step. I was greatly aided in my study from a book written in the 1800s by H. Clay Trumbull. His book entitled, *The Blood Covenant* was the only book I found that provided an in-depth study of universal covenant rituals.

When two Hebrews entered into a blood covenant, they went through a very specific ceremony. To explain it to you, I want to enter into this covenant with you. You and I are now going to enter into a blood covenant as two Hebrews would have done it.

Step 1. Take off Coat or Robe (1 Samuel 18:1-4)

The first thing I do is take off my coat or robe and give it to you. Now to the Hebrew, in a blood covenant ritual, a person's robe represents the person. By taking off my robe and giving it to you, I'm symbolically saying, *"I'm giving you all myself. My total being and my life, I pledge to you."* And then you would do the same to me.

Step 2. Take off Belt (1 Samuel 18:1-4)

The next thing I do is take off my belt and give it to you. Now I don't use my belt to hold up my pants, but to hold up my weapons. My belt holds my armor together; my dagger, my bow and arrow, my sword. So symbolically I'm giving you all my strength and pledging you all my support and protection. And as I give you my belt, I'm saying, *"Here is my strength and all my ability to fight. If anybody attacks you, they are also attacking me. Your battles are my battles and mine are yours. I will fight with you. I will help defend you and protect you."* And you do the same to me. This is similar to a compact nations might make today. But this one cannot be broken.

Step 3. Cut the Covenant (Genesis 15:1-9; Jeremiah 34:18-19)

The next step is to actually "cut the covenant" by taking an animal and splitting it right down the middle. In the Bible, an animal is only cut down the middle and split in two in a covenant ceremony.

After we split the animal, we lay each half to the side of us and stand in between the two bloody halves of flesh, with our backs to each other. Then we walk right through the bloody halves, making a figure eight, and come back to a stop facing each other.

In doing so we are saying two things. First, we are saying that we are dying to ourselves, giving up the rights to our own life and beginning a new walk with our covenant partner unto death. You see, in this covenant, each half of the dead animal represents us. And second, since the blood covenant is the most solemn pact, we each point down to the bloody animal split in two and say, "God do so to me and more if I ever try to break this covenant. Just split me right down the middle and feed me to the vultures because I tried to break the most sacred of all compacts."

Step 4. Raise the Right Arm and Mix Blood (Isaiah 62:8)

Then we raise our right arms, cut our palms and bring them together. As we do, our blood intermingles. Then we swear allegiance to each other.

Remember how you did that as a kid? With eyes probably half closed, you and your closest friend pricked your finger and brought them together swearing allegiance forever until mom broke the covenant for you.

As our blood intermingles, we believe our lives are intermingling and becoming one life. This is because our blood is our life and to intermingle blood is to intermingle life.

So we are putting off our old nature and putting on the nature of our blood covenant partner. We two are becoming one. Man has always believed that intermingling blood is intermingling life. This symbolically shows the two of us becoming one.

Step 5. Exchange Names (Genesis 17:5,15; 32:18)

Then as we stand there with our blood intermingling, we *exchange names.* I take your last name as part of my name, and you take my last name as part of your name.

Step 6. Make a Scar (Isaiah 49:16)

The next step is to rub our blood together and make a scar as a permanent testimony to the covenant. The scar will bear witness to the covenant we have made. It will always be there to remind us of our covenant responsibilities to each other. It is the guarantee of our covenant.

If anyone tries to harm us, all we have to do is raise up that right arm and show our scar. By that we are saying, "There's more to me than meets the eye. If you're coming after me, you're also going to have to fight my blood covenant partner. And you don't know how big he is. So what are you going to do? Are you going to take your chances or back off?" If the would be attacker has any sense, he's going to back off. So the scar is our seal that testifies to the covenant.

Henry Stanley, on his explorations through Africa, cut covenant 50 times with various chieftains. And we can certainly understand why. Anytime he would come across an unfriendly tribe, he would just hold up that right arm with those 50 scars and any would be attacker would take off running in the other direction. Today, when we meet friends, we don't show scars, we shake hands. There are many trappings of blood covenant in our modern society, we've just eliminated the blood.

Step 7. Give Covenant Terms (Genesis 31:52-53; 21:23; Joshua 9)

Then we stand before witnesses and give the *terms of the covenant*. I say, "All my assets are yours. All my money, all my property and all my possessions are yours. If you need any of them, you don't even have to ask. Just come and get it. What's mine is yours and what's yours is mine. And if I die, all my children are yours by adoption and you are responsible for my family."

But at the same time, you also get my liabilities. If I ever get in trouble financially, I don't come ask you for money. I come to you and say, "Where's our checkbook?"

We are in covenant. Everything I have is yours and yours is mine, both assets and liabilities. So we stand there and read off, before witnesses, our list of assets and liabilities.

Step 8. Eat Memorial Meal (Genesis 26:28-30; 31:44-54)

Then we have a *memorial meal* to complete the covenant union. In place of the animal and blood, we have bread and wine. In the Bible, wine is called the blood of the grapes (see Gen. 49:11) and it represents our own lifeblood. The bread represents our flesh.

We take a loaf of bread and break it in two and feed it to each other saying, "This is symbolic of my body and I'm now putting it in you." Then we serve each other wine and say, "This is symbolic of my lifeblood which is now your blood."

And now, symbolically, I'm in you and you're in me. We are now one together with a new nature.

Step 9. Plant a Memorial (Genesis 21:27-33; 31:44-54)

We now leave a *memorial to the covenant*. We want to always remember it. We do this by planting a tree that we have sprinkled with the blood of the animal. The blood-sprinkled tree, along with our scar, will always be a testimony to our covenant.

Well, this completes the ceremony. From now on, we are known as friends. In Bible times, one didn't use the word friend loosely as we do today. You became friends only after you had cut covenant. And all our children are included in this covenant, even the unborn ones. They are in covenant because they are in us. Later, when they are born and come to an age of understanding about our covenant, they can choose to stay in it, or reject it.

Identifying the Covenant

Now, anytime you see these happenings or these words referenced in the Bible, either actually or symbolically, you know the parties are entering into a blood covenant. You won't find all the details spelled out step by step as I have given them to you, because in Bible days everyone knew all the details and it wasn't necessary to record it all.

But get familiar with the nine steps and the covenant "lingo" because this is the basic ritual and you will want to recognize it as you read on and see how it is applied.

The Old Covenant

There are a number of examples of the blood covenant in the Bible. Abraham cut covenant with Abimelech, a Philistine king. Jacob cut covenant with Laban, his uncle. (see Genesis 21:21-34; 31:44-54.)

But the example I want to share with you is the covenant cut between David and Jonathan. The story begins in First Samuel 18:1-9 where we read the following account.

> *By the time David was through talking with Saul, Jonathan's soul was in unison with David's soul; Jonathan loved him as himself. On that same day Saul retained him and did not let him return to his father's home. Because he loved him, Jonathan made a covenant with David; he stripped himself of the robe he had on and gave it to David; also his armor with sword, bow, and belt. David went out wherever Saul sent him and enjoyed success, so that Saul put him in charge of troops, he was in favor with the people and with Saul's servants.*

Something happened, however, on their return trip from David's slaying of the Philistine. The women came out from all the Israelite towns to meet King Saul, singing and dancing to tambourines, and making joy with cymbals. As they danced, the women sang responsively, "Saul has slain his thousands and David his ten thousands." This made Saul very angry. The refrain disgusted him; he said to himself, "They ascribe to David ten thousands and to me only thousands; what more for him but the kingdom!" From that day on Saul kept an envious eye on David (1 Samuel 18:1-8).

Let's review the characters in this story.

David

David is the giant killer. He is the great warrior who could crush all his foes and all the enemies of Saul. And the Bible says that David is a man after God's own heart (Acts 13:22). David loves Saul. He has Saul's best interest at heart. David could have killed Saul on several occasions, but he kept forgiving him. David wants to show love to Saul but Saul won't let him.

Saul

Saul, on the other hand, is just the opposite of David. He has a knack for being outside the will of God. I can really identify with Saul. He is rebellious and seeks to do his own thing rather than God's thing. He doesn't want anybody telling him what to do, especially God. This rebelliousness continuously brings grief and sorrow to Saul.

Saul is afraid of David. This soon becomes an obsession to him so he hunts David down and tries to kill him. Saul makes everyone in his family afraid of David. The portrait he paints to his family is, "Big bad David is out to get us. Don't let him get too close or he'll kill you. He's mean and unjust and he'll destroy you if he gets the chance."

David, of course, is just the opposite of what Saul makes him out to be. But his family doesn't know any better and they're sure not going to get close enough to David to find out. They are afraid of David. They don't know David loves them.

Jonathan

Now, Saul has a son named Jonathan. Jonathan is just the opposite of Saul and the rest of the family. Although a member of the family of Saul, it's like he really doesn't belong there. He is more like David. In fact, Jonathan loves David as his own self. And, as we've just read, at a young age, Jonathan and David entered into a blood covenant.

Jonathan is always trying to bring peace between Saul and David. But the harder Jonathan tries, the angrier Saul becomes. At one point, in rage, Saul throws a spear at Jonathan, as he had David.

Mephibosheth

Later, when Jonathan marries, he has a son named Mephibosheth. In Second Samuel 4:4 we read that when Mephibosheth is five years old, Saul and Jonathan are killed in the battle at Jezreel.

This is terrible news. Not only because of their death, but, now with nobody to stop him, David can rush in and take over as king. And surely he will kill all of Saul's family who are left and all who are loyal to Saul because he hates Saul and wants to punish his household and bring destruction on them. Of course, David doesn't want to do this, but Saul's family believes he does.

So when the news of Saul and Jonathan's death reaches Jerusalem, Mephibosheth's nurse grabs him up and flees. In her haste to get away, she falls and drops Mephibosheth. As he hits the ground both feet are crushed. Quickly, the nurse picks him up and carries him to a hideout east of the Jordan River at Lo Debar. There, Mephibosheth takes refuge.

While hiding at Lo Debar, his heart hardens against David. His two lame feet are a constant reminder that David is out to get him; that David hates him and if David ever found him he would kill him. So instead of being in the comfortable palace with servants, roast duck for dinner, king size beds and silk sheets, Mephibosheth is hiding out like a runaway slave in fear of David. He doesn't know he is in covenant with the king through his father, Jonathan.

David Reigns as King

Meanwhile, David reigns as king. And in Second Samuel 9, we find David wondering if any of Saul's family is still alive. He wants to show them kindness because he is in covenant with Jonathan. But every time he approaches someone to ask about Jonathan's family, they say nothing. They believe David is just trying to trick them and if he ever found Mephibosheth, he would kill him.

But at last, a servant of Saul confides in David and tells him Mephibosheth is at Lo Debar. Immediately, David sends his chariots to get him. As Mephibosheth hears the roar in the distance, he pulls himself up to see what it is. His worst fears are confirmed...the chariots of David are coming to kill him.

When David's men arrive, they lift Mephibosheth into a chariot and rush him back to David. Mephibosheth naturally believes it is finally over for him. He's certain that David will torture him, behead him, and feed him to the dogs.

David Remembers Covenant

So as they hurry him into the palace before David, Mephibosheth falls down on his face before David. And just as he expects the guards to grab him, David says, "Mephibosheth, don't be afraid. I've asked you to come so I can be kind to you because of my covenant with your father, Jonathan. I will restore to you all the land of your grandfather, Saul, and you will live here at the palace."

Well, Mephibosheth can't believe his ears! This is the king who hates him and wants to kill him? He falls to the ground before David and cries out, "Should the king show kindness to a dead dog like me. You don't know what I've said about you. You don't know all the names I've called you; how I've hated you, made jokes about you and ran from you. I don't deserve any kindness or mercy. I'm worse than a dead dog fit only for the garbage heap. O Lord David. I'm not worthy of this love and mercy. I don't deserve such compassion and forgiveness."

David replies, "Mephibosheth, you don't understand. I know you don't deserve it. I know you don't merit it. And there is nothing you can do to earn or make up for your thoughts and actions against me. You could serve me a thousand years and never make it up. But this has nothing to do with you. Mephisosheth, you see this scar on my hand. I'm not doing this because of you. I'm doing this because I have sworn by my own blood and entered into an everlasting covenant with your father Jonathan. This scar in the palm of my hand is the guarantee and seal of the covenant.

"And here are the terms of the covenant. I will restore all your land. I will bless you. I'll forgive your past wrongs against me. My house is your house and you will live here at the palace. I'll be a father to you and adopt you as my own son. This scar is the testimony and witness to my covenant with you."

Mephibosheth Chooses

Naturally Mephibosheth is shaken. He can't believe it. But he must now make a choice, either to enter into the covenant with David or go back into the desert.

Doesn't sound like much of a choice, does it? Well, let's see. The man he has hated all his life he must now love with all his life. He must now become one with the man he ran away from and of whom he was afraid. He must swallow his pride and humble himself. He must admit he was wrong and turn his back on all his old ways of thinking about David. And his old friends will ridicule him, make fun of him, and call him a weakling for giving in to David. They will say he didn't have the guts enough to die and be done with.

Not such an easy decision after all, is it? Mephibosheth weighs the alternatives. It is his choice, his free will. David can't force the covenant on him. Gratefully, Mephibosheth chooses to enter the covenant with David.

Immediately, all the things David promised took place. Mephiposheth's land was restored. He was blessed with the blessings of a child of the king. All his past wrongs against David were forgiven. He joined David in a covenant meal, ate regularly at the king's table and lived at the king's palace. And the descendants of Mephibosheth were blessed because they too were in covenant; no one could harm them.

The New Covenant

Now this is a pretty story, but, "what does it have to do with my relationship with God?" In this story, David represents God.

He loves his creation with all His heart. He wants to show us mercy and kindness. He wants to take us out of the desert and wilderness of life and adopt us into His own family, to be His own children, to sit at the table with Him and live in a mansion He's prepared for us.

But unfortunately, we're in the family of Saul. And we're rebellious. We want to do our own thing. We don't want anybody telling us what to do, especially God. And we don't know God loves us and wants to bless us. We've always been told He is a God of wrath and wants to bring judgment on us. So we are afraid of Him. We run from Him and when we think He isn't looking, we laugh at Him, make fun of Him, and tell jokes about Him. We bring grief and sorrow on ourselves out in our own wilderness of Lo Debar.

What about Jonathan? He was in the family of Saul yet he didn't really belong there. He was like David who delighted to do the will of God. He was very Saul but also very David. Like Jesus, the Word of God who became flesh and dwelt among us, *Jesus didn't really fit in with us; yet He was one of us.* He was very God but at the same time, very man.

All the fullness of God dwelled in his body (see Col. 2:9). In Him is life and He is the source of life. Being God, all creation is in Him and comes from Him. As the Creator, He is worth all His creation. How many creatures are equal to the Creator? How many humans are equal to God? A thousand? A hundred thousand? A million? A billion?

All creatures put together don't equal the Creator. So if God became man, while at the same time, remaining God, He could stand in for all creation. He could represent all mankind. All humanity would be in Him. He could take the place of every person who ever lived. And being equal to God, even though a man, He could enter into covenant with Himself on behalf of all humanity.

Enter Jesus—the Perfect God-Man

Jesus is that perfect God-Man. The Bible says that it was decided on before the foundations of the world (see 1 Pet. 1:18-20). *And we were there when the covenant was cut because, as our Creator, we were in Him.*

And in God's own time, as He remembered the covenant that He made with Himself from the beginning, He came to the earth as one of us...flesh and blood and bones. He was born of the seed of woman, a virgin (see Gal. 4:4). He was born of the seed of woman, not man, so that the blood flowing through His veins would be uncontaminated by sin.

He didn't carry that deadly blood disease passed on by Adam called the sin nature (Romans 5:12). As God, He was perfectly holy and righteous. And He prepared for Himself a body. It was a body that would not know sin; therefore, the blood in that body was spotless and without blemish. So God, through the Son of God, exchanged names with us and became Jesus the human Son of Man...the representative of all mankind. He called Himself the Son of Man to identify Himself with all mankind. For 33 years He lived a perfect life in order to be the once and for all perfect sacrifice for the sins of the world.

Jesus Cuts Covenant

During the covenant ceremony, Jesus gathers His disciples together to participate in the covenant meal of bread and wine. After the meal Jesus went out and left a memorial to the covenant. He planted a tree. And He poured out blood on it. But it wasn't the blood of bulls and goats; it was His own blood. And it wasn't a little knick in His wrist. It was all His blood poured out at the foot of the Cross, the bloodstained tree that stands forever as a memorial to the covenant.

The "Lamb of God" slain from the foundations of the world cut covenant for all mankind. And we were there. We were crucified with Him, because like Mephibosheth, we were in Him as our Creator. He took on our robe of self-righteousness which is like filthy rags (Isaiah 64:6). He took on our nature. He took on all our liabilities which are the sins of our spirit, the sorrows of our soul and the sickness of our body. They were all placed on Him. All of our spiritual leprosy, that deadly blood disease we carry, was put on Him and He who knew no sin became sin for us (see Isa. 53:6).

It was necessary for God to do this because the sin nature within each of us separates us from God. All of us have sinned and come short of God's glory (see Rom. 3:23). The penalty for our sin is death (see Rom. 6:23). We all know this to be true which is why we are afraid of God. Jesus took all of this on Himself at the Cross.

Jesus Remembers Covenant

And somewhere you're sitting in church, or at home, or with a neighbor, at a bar, or at a Bible study, or at work, and the chariots of one greater than David, the Holy Spirit, invites you to come to God through His Son, Jesus. You've been fighting this all your life. You knew one day it was going to happen. But you've been running from it, hiding behind your mask of religion, drugs, sex, work, money, or something else to cover your trail. You thought God was out to get you and spoil your fun…to tell you not to do this or that or that or this.

You don't know that God loves you and wants to bless you with all spiritual blessings. So instead of living like a child of the king, you've been living like a runaway slave. You wouldn't believe those Christians who told you about the love of God. You thought they were trying to trick you, to get you to God so He could punish you. And so you've brought grief and sorrow on yourself and those around you.

But now the Holy Spirit is wooing you and convicting you. He's bringing you to God, and just as you think you're about to get it; just as you think the big heavenly club is about to come down on you, God says, "Don't be afraid. I've asked you to come so I can be kind to you because of the covenant I made with Myself on your behalf. I've been looking for you because I want to bless you."

You Must Choose

You can't believe your ears, "This is that great God of wrath who wants to punish me? This is the one I've been afraid of and running from all my life." You cry out, "But God, you don't know what I've said about You. You don't know how many times I've used your name in vain and how I've hated You and cursed You, made jokes about You and ran from You. Why, I even said You were dead. You just don't know all the terrible things I've done. I'm not worthy of this love and mercy. I don't deserve such compassion and forgiveness."

And God replies, "You don't understand. I know you don't deserve it. I know you can't make up for your thoughts and actions against Me. You could serve Me a thousand years and never make it up. But this has nothing to do with your deserving it. I'm doing this because I've sworn by My own blood and entered into an everlasting covenant with Myself on your behalf through Jesus. The nail scars in His hands are the guarantee and seal of the covenant. And you were there; you were in Me when I gave my life for you. Now I want to give My life to you."

Covenant Terms

God says, *"And here are the terms of the covenant. I'll take all your liabilities, all your sins, all your sorrows, all your sicknesses on Myself and become sin for you. I'll forgive your iniquities and remember them no more. I'll take all your self-righteousness and give you My own righteousness, which is pure and holy and acceptable to Me."*

like Hebrew covenant ritual

"You clothe Me with your robe of sin, sorrow, and heartache and I'll clothe you with My garment of salvation and My robe of righteousness which is My pure lifeblood poured out on the cross for you. I'll impute it to you and count you as righteous. We'll exchange natures. For I'll put My Spirit within you and bless you with all spiritual blessings. You'll partake of My own nature by the intermingling of our blood.

"You can become part of me and I'll live in your heart. My house will be your house. You can feast at My table. I'll be a Father to you and adopt you as My own child. You will reign with Me for a thousand years and have eternal life with Me. This is My free gift to you to show you that I love you." (See Jeremiah 31:31-34; Ezekiel 11:19-20; Ezekiel 36:25-28; Hebrews 8:8-12; Revelation 20:4; 22:1-5.)

Entering the Covenant

Well, this discovery undoes everything you ever thought about God. But you must make the choice. Your parents can't make it for you. Your religious organization can't make it for you. *You* must decide; either to enter into the covenant with God through Jesus or go back into the desert.

It's the same Jesus you may have been running from all your life. The one you've mocked all your life. You must now love with all your life. You must now become one with Jesus. You must swallow all your pride, humble yourself, and admit you were wrong, turning your back on your old way of thinking and living. And all your old friends will ridicule you, make fun of you, and call you names for following Jesus.

This is certainly not an easy decision. If you decide no; you go back into the desert, lost forever. If you decide yes; you will have communion with God and feed on his very divine nature. He will be your God and you will be His people.

And Jesus says, "If you enter into the covenant, you'll be known as my friend." (see John 15:14-15.) You'll even exchange names and be called a Christian, believer, disciple, etc.

Jesus said,

> ...unless you eat the flesh of the Son of Man and drink his blood, you have no life in you; he who eats my flesh and drinks my blood has eternal life and I will raise him up at the last day. For my flesh is food indeed, and my blood is drink indeed. He who eats my flesh and drinks my blood abides in me and I in him. As the living Father has sent me, and I live because of the Father, so he who eats me will live because of me (John 6:53-57 RSV).

Jesus further explains that these words He is speaking are spiritual words of *spiritual things* for divine human union is spiritual (see John 6:63). You see, God is a spirit and to worship Him you must worship Him in spirit (see John 4:24). You must be born again spiritually (see John 3:1-7). That's how we become one with God through Jesus.

Supernatural Scar

Like the scar, Jesus sends the Holy Spirit to all who will enter into covenant with Him (see John 20:22). The Holy Spirit is the seal that bears witness and testifies to the covenant. He is the constant reminder, the guarantee that we are in covenant with God through the blood of Jesus. (see Eph. 1:13; 4:30; 2 Cor. 1:22).

Romans 8:14-17 (KJV) says it this way, "For as many as are led by the Spirit of God, they are the sons of God. For ye have not received the spirit of bondage again to fear; but we have received the spirit of adoption, whereby we cry, Abba, Father (our dear Heavenly Father). The Spirit itself beareth witness with our spirit, that we are the children of God: and if children, then heirs; heirs of God, and joint heirs with Christ...."

Showing the Scar

So when satan, the enemy, comes against the believer, we show him our scar...the power of the Holy Spirit. You see, greater is He who is in us (the Holy Spirit) than he (satan) who is in the world (see 1 John 4:4). *And when satan sees our scar, he will flee from us because he knows he has already been whipped by our blood covenant brother, Jesus of Nazareth, the Son of the Living God.*

For God has raised and exalted Jesus and placed Him above all principalities and powers with authority over every name that is named (see Eph. 1:20-23). He has given Jesus "The Name", and "The Name" is above every name (see Phil. 2:9-11). Believers have the authority to go into the world in "The Name" through the power of the Holy Spirit. We are more than conquerors through Jesus as we go in His name; for all things are under His feet and we become part of His body through spiritual union (see Rom. 8:37; Eph. 1:20-23).

And as you go in "The Name", the God of peace, who brought again from the dead, the Lord Jesus, that great shepherd of the sheep, through the blood of the everlasting covenant, will produce in you through the power of Jesus all that is pleasing to Him (see Heb. 13:20-21).

The Covenant Invitation

Jesus now stands knocking at the door of every human heart. He desires that all will enter into blood covenant with Him by personally accepting His death on their behalf. This is His covenant of love. For all who will enter into the covenant, He promises, "…I will come in to him and eat with him and he with Me" (Rev. 3:20 RSV).

If you have not yet entered into this covenant of love, you may do so right now, right where you are. You simply confess to God that you are a sinner and that you cannot save yourself. You then enter into the covenant by asking Jesus to come into your life and be your personal Lord and Savior.

At that point, God accepts you in the covenant through Jesus who sends the Holy Spirit to live His life in you. The Holy Spirit will bear witness to your own human spirit that you have now entered into the covenant and become a child of God. Then ask God to fill you with His Holy Spirit for power to live a victorious life.

Anyone may pray this prayer. There is no difference between Jew and Gentile. The same Lord is Lord of all and gives His blessings to all who call upon Him. For everyone who calls upon the name of the Lord shall be saved. (see Romans 10:12-13.)

God progressively reveals this invitation throughout the Old Covenant, which is but a shadow pointing us to the New

Covenant light of the world, Jesus the One and Only True Messiah, Lord and Savior. We join Him now in Chapter 3 as He calls one man into His covenant of love.

Chapter 3

WHAT DID ABRAHAM BELIEVE?

Background

With Chapter 2 as our background, we're now going to study the blood covenant as God revealed it through Abram, later called Abraham after the covenant was established.

It's been 500 years since the flood and again the world has turned from God to idol worship. Abram's family were idol worshipers (Joshua 24:2,14). They lived in the city of Ur, located in Babylon between the Tigris and Euphrates Rivers. It was a cultural, sophisticated, but pagan country. The people worshiped the moon and made idols carved with their own hands to the moon goddess.

From this environment, God called Abram to His covenant of love. God told Abram to get out of his pagan land. Abram was to leave his idols and his pagan household and go to a country that God would show him. There God would bless him and make him a great nation. God would give Abram a land of rest from his enemies. And out of Abram's seed (singular) all nations of the world would be blessed. (see Genesis 12:1-9.)

Four times the Bible says that Abraham believed God and was counted as righteous (see Gen. 15:6; Rom. 4:3; Gal. 3:6; James 2:23). What we are going to learn in this chapter is exactly...*What was it Abraham believed?* If we can find out what Abraham believed, then, we too can be counted as righteous, if we choose to believe it. We too can become acceptable to God. We too can be reconciled with our Creator. We can have peace with God.

So God brings Abram to the land of Canaan and God approaches him in a way that Abram can understand. He established a blood covenant with Abram. It's the same covenant he established with Adam and Eve when he killed the animals in the garden, clothed Adam and Eve to cover their sin and promised a future redeemer. (see Genesis 3.) It's the same covenant God reconfirmed with Noah, evidenced by Noah offering a sacrifice to the Lord that was a sweet savory smell. (see Genesis 8:20-21.) That's the first thing Noah did as soon as he got off the boat. And I don't blame him.

The Old Covenant

And so God progressively continues to reveal His covenant with man that He (God) laid from the foundations of the world. And before He actually comes to earth to cut covenant Himself as a man, He reveals it most clearly through Abraham. The covenant ceremony is described in Genesis 15 and reads as follows:

> *After these things the word of the Lord came unto Abram in a vision saying, Fear not, Abram: I am thy shield, and thy exceeding great reward...and he said unto him, Take me an heifer of three years old, and a she goat of three years old, and a ram of three years old, and a turtledove and a young pigeon. And he took unto him all these, and divided them in the midst, and laid each piece one against another: but the birds divided he not. And when the fowls came down upon the carcasses, Abram drove them away. And when the sun was going down, a deep sleep fell upon Abram; and, lo, an horror of great darkness fell upon him. And he said unto Abram, Know of a surety that thy seed shall be a stranger in a land that is not theirs, and shall serve them; and they shall afflict them four hundred years. And also that nation, whom they shall serve, will I judge: and afterward shall they come out with great substance.*

> *And thou shalt go to thy fathers in peace; thou shall be buried in a good old age. But in the fourth generation they shall come hither again: for the iniquity of the Amorites is not yet full. And it came to pass, that, when the sun went down, and it was dark, behold a smoking furnace, and a burning lamp that passed between those pieces. In the same day the LORD made*

a covenant with Abram, saying, Unto thy seed have I given this land, from the river of Egypt unto the great river, the river Euphrates (Genesis 15:1,9-18 KJV).

Ceremony Described

Let's review. God says, "Abram, I am your shield and your exceeding great reward." With this statement, God is taking the initiative by offering His robe and His belt to Abram. (This is according to the covenant ceremony discussed in Chapter 2.) Now God doesn't have a physical robe that He exchanges with Abram. But since the robe represents the person, God simply offers Himself.

In effect, God says, "Abram, here is Myself. I offer you Me. I am your reward. All that I am, I give to you. I am holy; I give you My holiness. I am righteous; I give you My righteousness. I give you My life, Abram, pledging to lay it down on your behalf if you will accept this covenant and enter into it with Me."

Then God says, "Abram, I am your shield. I don't offer you a shield: I am your shield. I will protect you and fight your battles for you. I will be your strength. If anyone attacks you, they are really attacking Me. Your battles are Mine. Put Me on as your full armor. And when you go into battle, I'll fight for you. You just stand aside and let Me do it.

"And out of your seed (singular) shall come a blessing to the whole world. I will bless you and make you a great nation. I will give you a land of rest. But Abram, I want you to know I'm not making this covenant with you because you deserve it. Your self-righteousness is like filthy rags to Me. And anytime you start thinking you do deserve it, we'll go ask your wife, whom you gave away two times, what she thinks. I'm taking the initiative to make this covenant with you because I love you, not because you deserve it."

Abram, that great man of faith, responds, "Well, that's really wonderful, Lord. I really appreciate all you want to do for me and I believe you, Lord. I know you are going to do all that, but how do I know?"

Well, God answers Abram's question in terms Abram can understand. He tells Abram to gather up some animals; a heifer, a goat, a ram, a turtledove, and a young pigeon. These are animals God has declared as "clean" or acceptable to Him. They would serve as substitutionary sacrifices leading up to the ultimate sacrifice.

And so, Abram quickly gathers up the animals and God says, "Take the ram, goat, and heifer and split them right down the middle and separate the halves."

By splitting the animals down the middle and dividing the halves, Abram knows that God is making a covenant with him. And Abram knows that a blood covenant is the closest, the most enduring, the most solemn and the most sacred of all compacts. It absolutely cannot be broken. Therefore, Abram knows that God must do the things He has promised.

No need for Abram to worry and fret about it. He can rest on God's promises, because through the blood covenant, he has a binding connection to God.

There's only one problem. How can the creation enter into covenant with the Creator? How can weak sinful man enter into covenant with the all-mighty, all-powerful God? What does Abram have to offer God? Is he going to rescue God and help Him out in some way? Why, if every human that ever lived offered all their possessions to God, it still wouldn't be worthy of a covenant.

The Creator is beyond reach of the creation in the creation's own capacity to reach out. There's just no common ground on which man can approach God.

But in Genesis 15:11 we see Abram trying to help God. As the bloody halves of the animals lay there separated, fowls swoop down and try to devour the carcasses. These fowls are considered unclean by God and they attempt to eat the clean sacrifice ordained by God as acceptable to Him.

Jesus says satan, the evil one, is like the unclean fowls that swoop down to snatch away the seeds of the gospel to keep people from believing (see Matt. 13:4,19). The fowls in Genesis represent satan swooping down to break up this covenant before it is completed by snatching away the acceptable sacrifice before it can be offered. So we see Abram trying to help God out by shooing them away.

Finally God says, "Look, Abram, you really don't understand. If I'm going to establish a covenant with man; I'm going to have to do it all if it's going to be done at all. If you are involved in this in anyway, it's going to be messed up. If you try to work, if you try to be righteous, if you try to help in any way, this covenant will be polluted with you. And then it won't be acceptable to Me. I'm the only one who can make a covenant with Me. I'm going to swear by Myself to this covenant. And to make sure you don't try to help Me out anymore, I'm going to put you to sleep through the whole ceremony. And when it's over, I'll wake you up."

So God caused a deep sleep to fall upon Abram and there was a great darkness. While Abram was under the power of God, God told Abram his descendants would be in bondage 400 years in a strange country, but they would be delivered with great wealth.

Then Abram saw passing between the bloody animals, someone taking his place. Someone was walking where he should have been walking. Someone was saying, "I'm dying to myself. I'm giving up the rights to my own life. I'm beginning a new walk with my covenant partner unto death."

Remember the covenant partner here is God. So someone is saying, "Not my will God, but yours be done as my covenant partner." It was such a brilliant glow that Abram saw walking in his place, that he could only describe it as a smoking furnace and a burning lamp, meaning a bright light. *What was it Abram saw?*

Abram sees a manifestation of the blazing glory and dazzlingly beauty of God Himself walking in his place. The Almighty cut covenant with Himself and stood in for Abram. *He is the only one who could stand in for Abram.* And all of Abram's unborn seed were included in the covenant because they were in Abram.

Once again we see how the Old Testament is a picture of a person in the New Testament. God pictured the time when He would come to earth in the person of Jesus of Nazareth to cut a covenant with Himself by Himself on our behalf.

The Sacrifice, remember, was always symbolic of the flesh and blood of the one who made the walk. So this sacrifice pointed to the time when God Himself would come to earth as the human "Lamb of God" to take away the sins of the world. He would cut the covenant for us. While the blood of animals could only cover sin, the blood of Jesus takes it away to be remembered no more.

Seal of Circumcision

Then, in Genesis 17, God awakens Abram to seal the covenant. The seal, as we discussed in Chapter 2, is the scar given as the testimony to the covenant. The scar would bear witness to the covenant. It would always remind God and Abram of their covenant responsibilities to each other. It was the guarantee of the covenant.

The scar that sealed and testified to this covenant was circumcision. It was the token of the everlasting covenant. Abram would bear in his flesh, the evidence that he had entered into blood covenant with God through Jesus. All of Abram's natural descendants would confirm their accepting the covenant by taking the seal of circumcision on newborn males. In this way, the seal, the reminder, the testifier to the covenant was passed down.

Change of Names

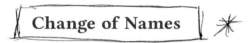

Then according to covenant ritual, God and Abram changed names. God, who is called YHWH in Hebrew, took the "H" out of his own name and put it in Abram's name. So Abram's name was changed to Abraham. Likewise, Sara's name is changed to Sarah. God took on Abraham's name and became known as the God of Abraham. And now that the covenant is cut, they are known as friends. Abraham is to be known as the friend of God. (see James 2:23.)

But Abraham Has No Son

Abraham is now the covenant friend of God. And God has promised him a seed (singular) through Sarah, a descendant who would be a blessing to the whole world. He has also promised him a land of rest and blessing upon Abraham and his descendants. There's only one problem with all these promises, Abraham has no son through Sarah. Abraham had earlier given birth to Ishmael through Hagar, Sarah's handmaiden. But the promised seed was to come through Sarah. Now he's 100 years old and Sarah is

90. He's impotent and she is past the age of child bearing. God is a little more polite in describing their condition. He says they are stricken with age. (see Genesis 18:11).

So we see if Abraham is going to have a son, it will definitely have to be a supernatural birth. God is asking Abraham to believe in a supernatural birth. Now Abraham has never had a covenant partner like God before. It takes him a while to get used to the level and magnitude of promises coming from having such a partner. It's just not everybody you cut covenant with that delivers in the divine style.

But Abraham finally comes to the persuasion that God is bound to the covenant and can't break it. So He has to deliver. Furthermore, since He is God, He's also capable of delivering. So a son is born to Abraham through Sarah and he's called Isaac. (see Genesis 21:5.) God is living up to His part of the covenant.

Abraham's Test of Faith

But you recall Abraham slept through the covenant. God did it all. Abraham had nothing to do with it. God is proving Himself faithful so now it's time to test Abraham's faithfulness to the covenant. Did he really believe in his heart? Or was it just mental assent, and empty ritual he was going through.

Remember that when a covenant is cut, each party completely surrenders himself in loving trust to the other party. He must be willing to give his total being, his total life, his total heart to the one he is in covenant with. It is a dying to one's self and a surrender of yourself to the one you are in covenant with. *The blood covenant is not a mere intellectual understanding between Abraham and God, or you and God.*

The Test

There is only one way to find out Abraham's commitment to the covenant. That way is to test Abraham with that which is most dear to him...his only son.

All over the world, men in blood covenant were willing to give that which was most dear to them. Devotees of pagan gods would give their firstborn. This was common practice.

Would Abraham do the same for his God? God is asking Abraham, "Do you love Me as much as the heathens do their idols? Are you willing to surrender that which is most dear to you to prove that you love Me, or was it just easy talk? Have you really given Me your heart, Abraham? Or was the covenant something you agreed to for reasons that were not pure? Abraham, take your son, Isaac, your only son whom you love more than anything in the world, take Isaac to the land of Moriah and offer him to Me as a burnt offering. Abraham, it's a three-day journey. When you get there, I'll point out the mountain you are to offer him upon." (see Genesis 22:1-2.)

Well, this is a tough test for Abraham even though offering the firstborn was common practice. Because Abraham is 100 years old and all the promises God gave depend solely on him having a son. And at the age of 100, Abraham probably thinks there's not much hope of having another son. After all, Abraham reasons, "God is still tired from the miracle with Isaac and that took him 25 years." And by the time another 25 years roll along, Abraham figures he'll surely be too old for God to do anything with.

I'm sure these thoughts flashed through Abraham's mind. I know they would have mine. But Romans 4:20 says, "Abraham staggered not at the promises of God."

For a Middle-Easterner, like Abraham, to offer his only son's life was a far greater sacrifice than offering his own life. If God had asked Abraham to offer himself, a tired, worn out old man of 100, it would not have been a true test of Abraham's faithfulness to the covenant. But for Abraham to offer his only son and once again become childless at such an old age…this is the ultimate sacrifice. You see, in the Middle-Eastern mind, to die without a son was the most terrible thing in life. Your whole life would be considered a failure. The saying in those days was, "Heaven awaits not one who is destitute of a son." So in offering his only son, Abraham would prove in the most supreme way that he loved God and would be faithful to the covenant. God was not asking Abraham to do anything others would not do for their pagan gods.

Abraham Offers Isaac

Abraham arises early the next morning to begin his *three-day journey* toward a mountain at a city called Salem, later to be called Jerusalem. Abraham saddled a donkey and took Isaac and two servants with him. For the three-day journey to that mountaintop, in Abraham's mind, Isaac is as good as dead. This journey is described in Genesis 22.

On the third day of the journey, God points out Mount Moriah where Isaac is to be sacrificed. Abraham then turns to the servants and says, "Stay here with the donkeys. The lad and I will travel yonder and worship and then come right back" (Gen. 22:5 TLB).

Then Abraham places the wood for the burnt offering upon Isaac's shoulders and the two of them go on together. I agree with Jewish teachings that Isaac is a young man in his early thirties, (probably 33.) The Jewish age of maturity was 30. Isaac didn't marry until he was 40 and he had no children until he was 60. So even at 33 he would be considered a young man. So Isaac had three years of manhood before he was offered as a sacrifice.

On the way to the top of Mount Moriah, Isaac turns to Abraham and says, "Father we have the wood and the flint to make the fire, but where is the lamb for the sacrifice?" (Gen. 22:7 TLB).

Abraham replies, "God will provide Himself the lamb for a burnt offering" (v. 8). From this statement, we realize that Abraham believed God would provide a *substitute sacrifice on his behalf.* Hebrews 11:19 tells us Abraham believed that even if God did take Isaac, He would resurrect him to be the firstborn of the covenant children God promised Abraham. Abraham also believed he would have many children thereafter through the seed of Isaac.

So Abraham builds the altar and places Isaac on it. Just as he is about to make the sacrifice and take his own son's life, God steps in and says, "Abraham, you've proven your faithfulness to the covenant. Take this ram I have provided and offer him in place of your son. I will accept him as a substitute sacrifice in our covenant" (vv. 11-12).

Abraham offered up the ram and named the mountain, The Lord will provide, and it is said on this mountain, it (the sacrifice) shall be provided, it will be seen" (v. 14). The Revised Standard Version of the Bible has a footnote to this passage that reads, "He will be seen."

A Bride Is Chosen

Seven years later after the substitute sacrifice is made, Eliezer, Abraham's servant, seeks out a bride for Isaac. He finds Rebekah and brings her out of the slavery to sinful idol worship in the city of Haran and brings her into the Promised Land to begin a new life with Isaac. (see Genesis 24.)

In Review

So God cut covenant with Abraham. Satan tried to devour the acceptable sacrifice before the covenant could be completed. And God had to put Abraham to sleep to keep him from interfering. If Abraham tried to approach God on his own and help Him out, there could be no covenant made. It was all God's doings... strictly an act of grace and mercy on His behalf.

God took Abraham's place in the covenant ceremony. This was necessary because only God could enter into covenant with God. Abraham did nothing but believe. But he did act on his belief with deeds. God stood in for Abraham and walked in his place representing him in the covenant. The covenant was sealed by circumcision. Abram became Abraham, the friend of God. God became the God of Abraham. Abraham believed God and because of his belief, God counted him as righteous.

What Did Abraham Believe?

So what was it Abraham believed?

1. First of all, he believed in a *supernatural birth*. He believed God would supernaturally bring a son into the world. God did and Abraham called him Isaac.

2. He believed God enough to offer his only son as a sacrifice. And he did.

3. He believed for *three days* that his son was as good as dead. And he was.

4. He believed God would provide a sacrifice subsititute or *raise his son from the dead* with many children coming to him through his son Isaac. And God did.

5. He believed on that very mountain, *God would provide Himself* the substitute sacrifice…He would be seen on that very mountain.

And because Abraham believed these things in his heart, God gave Abraham His (God's) own robe of righteousness. Because of Abraham's faith, God was his shield, his protection. The righteousness of God was imputed or counted to Abraham's behalf because he believed.

The New Covenant

Jesus, speaking to the Jewish leaders said, "Your father Abraham rejoiced that he was to see my day; he saw it and was glad" (John 8:56 RSV). The apostle Paul writes that the gospel was preached to Abraham (see Gal. 3:8) and in Romans 9:8 Paul writes, "*…not all of Abraham's children are the children of God, but only those who believe the promise of salvation He made to Abraham.*"

God asks us to believe the same thing he asked Abraham to believe. He asks us to believe that Jesus, the Son of God, has entered into a covenant with God the Father on our behalf. We are separated from God by our sin and there's no way we can shoo away the fowls ourselves; meaning, there's nothing we can do to reconcile ourselves to God. There is no good work we can do to earn our way into the covenant. We can't help God out with our own righteousness. In fact, the only way we can come into the covenant is to confess helplessness before God and accept the one who walked in our place as Abraham did.

A Supernatural Birth

So first, we are asked to believe in a supernatural birth. As with Abraham, God would bring his only begotten Son into the world in the flesh, supernaturally. He would be born of a virgin...the seed of woman, thus not inheriting man's sin nature passed down from Adam. God did, and He called His name Jesus (Yeshua). (See John 1:1, 14; Luke 1:30-35.) Jesus was circumcised on the eighth day to prove he was still honoring the covenant. (See Luke 2:21.)

And satan was there trying to swallow up and devour the sacrifice before the covenant could be completed. Through Herod's mass murders, satan tried to kill Jesus when Jesus was still a baby. His parents, Joseph (Yosef) and Mary (Miriam), fled to Egypt and escaped. Satan again tried to kill Jesus, this time in the wilderness. He tried to have Jesus stoned and thrown off the cliff. All of these attempts on Jesus' life were to stop the covenant from being completed.

Keeping the Covenant Promise

But God had promised Abraham that in his seed, all nations of the earth would be blessed. And now it's time for God to prove His fidelity to the covenant with Abraham and Abraham's seed.

Like Abraham, Jesus had two of His disciples get a donkey for Him to ride into Jerusalem (see Mattthew 21:1-7). Then at the age of 33, after three years of ministering, Jesus began a long climb to the top of a mountain. And like Abraham, God placed the wood for the burnt offering on His Son's shoulders. That wood was the cross that Jesus voluntarily took on Himself. God offered His only Son as a burnt offering to be a blessing to the whole world.

When we, like Isaac, turn to God and ask, "Where is the sacrifice? Who will take my place and be my sin substitute? Who will pay the penalty for me?" The answer comes back, *"God will provide Himself the lamb for a burnt offering." Jesus is the "Lamb of God." But where Isaac was not worthy and needed a substitute for himself, Jesus is worthy. All the fullness of God dwelled in Him bodily.* (see Col. 1:19; 2:9.) God truly did provide Himself.

The Perfect Substitute

God Himself climbed up on that altar of the Cross on the same mountain where Isaac was offered 2,000 years earlier. But this time God did not stop the sacrifice, because the real substitute was already on the altar. Jesus is the "Lamb of God" slain from the foundations of the world and now He's come to shed His blood in fulfillment of the covenant. This is the covenant He swore by Himself to make from the beginning.

On that same mountain where Isaac was offered, the Lord did provide Himself as the substitute, and He was seen by the whole world. As with Abraham, a great darkness fell upon the earth. (see Matthew 27:45.) And so we are asked to believe that God sent His only Son to sacrifice Himself as our sin offering substitute.

Jesus the Resurrection

Next we are asked to believe that after Jesus was in the grave for three days and three nights, God the Father resurrected Him to be the firstborn of the covenant children of God, and many would come thereafter through Jesus. We even change our name and are called Christians, or believers, or disciples, etc. Jesus becomes our friend, our covenant partner.

The Heavenly Bride

And seven weeks after the substitutionary sacrifice, the Holy Spirit comes to begin His work of seeking the Bride for Jesus. He wants to deliver you from your slavery to sin and bring you into the promised land of spiritual rest with Jesus. Jesus is the heavenly Bridegroom and He seeks you for a Bride.

All the while, satan is there trying to keep you from entering the covenant. His words are very familiar to us, "You don't need all that blood business. You are a good person, an outstanding member of your community and a fine church worker. Why, your morals are much better than your neighbors. And it's all relative anyway. Surely a loving God wouldn't turn you away. So go ahead and do your own thing. After all, God helps those who help themselves. So if it feels good, do it."

These are lies of satan who disguises himself as an angel of light. But in actuality, he wants to devour you like a roaring lion and sift you as wheat.

But the Holy Spirit brings you to Jesus who says, "I am the way, the truth, and the life: no man comes to the Father, but by me. The penalty for sin is death and without the shedding of blood there is no forgiveness of sin. And it's my blood you must accept on your behalf to become covenant children of God." (see John 14:6; Romans 3:23; 6:23.)

The Real Children of Abraham

We see that Abraham is the spiritual father of all who believe as he believed. Jesus said that the *real* children of Abraham do the works of Abraham (see John 8:39). Again, Jesus said that the work of Abraham is *that he believed the witness of God to His Son* (see John 6:29; Romans 3-4; Galatians 3:6-9.)

When we believe what Abraham believed, the righteousness of Jesus is imputed or counted to us. We put on the robe of the Lord Jesus and His righteousness. We are the righteousness of God in Him. (see 2 Corinthians 5:21.) When God looks at us, He doesn't see us in our sin, He sees us in His Son. He sees us with the righteousness of Jesus. He becomes our shield and the full armor of our salvation. He is our exceedingly great reward.

The Child of God

We become spiritual children of God by faith in Jesus (see Galatians 3:26); *not evidenced by a circumcision of the flesh, but a circumcision of the heart.* This happens when Jesus puts His Spirit within us. (see John 20:22.)

When the Holy Spirit comes to live in us, He brings with Him spiritual blessings and a promised land of rest for our souls in God through Jesus who is our rest.

It is the Holy Spirit within us who is greater than he (satan) who is in the world. He is our source of strength. He fights our battles for us. He cleanses us of sin. When He fills us with His presence, we experience His love, His joy, His peace, His power, His grace, His glory, and His life flowing through us.

When Jesus said, "I am come that they might have life and that they might have it more abundantly," (John 10:10 KJV)

He was talking about *His life* living in us through the person of the Holy Spirit. Therefore, we can do all things through Jesus our Lord who strengthens us (Phil. 4:13). While there is a literal Promise Land (Israel), this is a spiritual promise land of rest God has made available to all of us. All who will may walk in this land by entering into the blood covenant with God through Jesus.

Entering Into the Covenant

God desires to count you as righteous, just as He did Abraham. He wants to bless you with all spiritual blessings. He wants you to partake of His very own divine nature. But you must say "yes" to the covenant. You must agree with God that you are separated from Him by your sins, and that there's nothing you can do to earn your way into the covenant. You then take Jesus into your life accepting Him as the one who made the covenant walk for you, just as Abraham did.

When you enter into the covenant, the spiritual promises made to Abraham become rightfully yours. "For we are the circumcision, which worship God in the spirit, and rejoice in Christ [Messiah] Jesus, and have no confidence in the flesh" (Phil. 3:3 KJV). "For he is not a Jew, which is one outwardly; neither is that circumcision, which is outward in the flesh; But he is a Jew, which is one inwardly; and circumcision is that of the heart, in the spirit, and not in the letter; whose praise is not of men, but of God" (Rom. 2:29 KJV). (See also Deuteronomy 10:16; 30:6; Jeremiah 4:4; 9:25-26; Galatians 6:15; 2 Corinthians 5:17.)

Paul did not mean that there are not ethnic Jews nor did he mean that Gentile believers become Jews. He was simply stating that true circumcision is of the heart and everyone whose heart has been circumcised is a true son and daughter of Abraham either by natural birth (Jewish believers) or spiritual birth (Gentile believers).

The covenant of love through the blood of Messiah Yeshua brings both Jew and Gentile into union with God. We both become one new man in Jesus. Through Him, we all have access by the Holy Spirit to God as our Heavenly Father. Therefore, "There is neither Jew nor Greek, there is neither bond nor free, there is neither male nor female: for ye are all one in Christ Jesus. And if ye be Christ's, then ye are Abraham's seed, and heirs according to the promise" (Gal. 3:28-29 KJV).

If you have just now entered into the covenant, I have the authority by the Word of God, to tell you that your sins are now forgiven never to be remembered again (John 20:23). Welcome to the family of God. Now go tell someone of your decision.

Chapter 4

THE TABERNACLE

Background

In Chapter 3, we learned how God reconfirmed His covenant with Abraham promising to come to the earth and cut the covenant through the seed (singular) of Abraham. But first Abraham's descendants would be in bondage for 400 years (see Gen. 15:13-36) in a strange land, Egypt. But this is a blood covenant and God must honor it. He must bring them out of bondage into the land of promise.

How God remembered the covenant is recorded in Exodus 2-3. Exodus 2:23-24 says, "In the course of those many days the king of Egypt died. And the people of Israel groaned under their bondage, and cried out for help, and their cry under bondage came up to God. And God heard their groaning, and God remembered His covenant with Abraham, Isaac and Jacob" (RSV).

Later, God miraculously appears to Moses to reveal His plan for deliverance. God tells Moses, "...I am the God of your father, the God of Abraham, the God of Isaac, and the God of Jacob...."

Then God said,

> *...I have seen the afflictions of my people who are in Egypt, and have heard their cry because of their taskmasters; I know their sufferings, and I have come down to deliver them out of the hand of the Egyptians, and to bring them up out of that land to a good and broad land, a land flowing with milk and honey, to the place of the Canaanites, the Hittites, the Ammonites, the Perizzites, the Hivites, and the Jebusites. And now, behold, the cry of the people of Israel has come to me and I have seen the oppression with which the Egyptians oppress them. Come, I will send you to Pharaoh that you may bring forth my people, the sons of Israel, out of Egypt* (Exodus 3:6-11 RSV).

God is honoring His covenant with Abraham. With a great show of power, He delivers this nation of several million. The final escape brought about by His parting the Red Sea for the Hebrews to pass through.

God's Calling Card

But along the way to their new land, God realizes that Abraham's descendants don't really understand who they are in covenant with. They don't realize how sinful they are and how holy He is. Later, through the prophet Jeremiah, God would say,

"The heart is deceitful above all things, and desperately wicked: who can know it" (Jeremiah 17:9 KJV).

Well, to bring this to their attention, God speaks to the Hebrew people as they journey and says, "Let's just pause here for a while at the foot of this mountain and let Me introduce Myself."

Exodus 19:17-18 reads, "Then Moses led the people out of the camp to meet God and they stood at the base of the mountain. All of Mount Sinai was smoking, because the Lord came down upon it in fire; its smoke went up like the smoke of a furnace and the whole mountain quaked severely" (MLB) Notice that Moses describes the covenant-keeping God in the same way Abraham did..."a smoking furnace."

God needs some way to introduce Himself; some *calling card* He can give the Hebrews to let them know what His character is and what He is really like. So He booms out the Ten Commandments..."Thou shalt have no other Gods before Me...Thou shalt not make unto thee any graven image nor bow down to them... Thou shalt not take the name of the Lord thy God in vain... Remember the Sabbath day, to keep it holy...Honor thy father and thy mother... Thou shalt not kill...Thou shalt not commit adultry...Thou shalt not steal...Thou shalt not bear false witness against thy neighbor...Thou shalt not covet anything that is thy neighbor's." (see Exodus 20.)

Wow! What a covenant partner. That's some calling card. Of course, God never expected the Hebrews to keep these commandments. He knew they couldn't because of that sin nature within them. *The commandments were to be a mirror for the people to see how holy He is and how sinful they are.* Then when the people see who He really is, they'll fall down before Him in worship, praise, and thanksgiving for His great grace and mercy to enter into covenant with them.

The Covenant Reconfirmed

To make this clear, along with giving the Ten Command-ments, God gave some additional directions. He gave special instructions for building a *Tabernacle*, for establishing an elaborate system of *sacrifices*, and for ordaining a *priesthood*. After receiving these instructions, Moses built an altar and offered a sacrifice to God. He took the blood of the sacrificed animals and splashed it against the altar. Then after publicly reading the Ten Command-ments and other laws before the nation, he threw blood toward the people themselves. In the same manner, he sprinkled blood over the Book of the Covenant containing the Ten Command-ments and all the laws.

Later he would sprinkle blood over the Tabernacle and all its furnishings used in worship as well as those who would minister as priests. (see Hebrews 9:18-22.) Then Moses said, "...This blood (not the Ten Commandments) confirms and seals the covenant the Lord has made with you in giving you these laws" (Exodus 24:8 TLB).

You see God never intended the Hebrews to approach Him by trying to keep the Ten Commandments. The Ten Commandments can't offer the blood evidence of a life given. God intended the Hebrews to approach Him the way He had always intended... through a *blood sacrifice for the forgiveness of sin.* That's His provi-sion. That's His *only* provision.

The Hebrew word for Law is *Torah*. This word simply means teaching or instruction. God's Ten Commandments and Laws were instructions to the Hebrews on how to approach Him. You see, God had in mind that when the Hebrew heard the Ten Com-mandments he would run as fast as he could to the Tabernacle, kill a lamb, and offer the blood in his place as a substitute sin offering to a holy God.

Therefore God established a Tabernacle, a sacrifice system and a priesthood as the way for the Hebrew to approach Him. *The Hebrew was not to approach God by The Ten Commandments but through the sacrifices administered by the priest at the Tabernacle.* In Psalm 50:5, God reminded His people that He entered into covenant with them by sacrifice.

Christian ministers usually teach that, in the Old Testament, the Jews were saved by the Law but that has been replaced by grace and mercy in the New Testament. This is just not true. Everyone who has ever approached God had to do so in faith in the the grace and mercy of God provided by the blood of the innocent substitutionary sacrifice for their sins.

The Old and the New

Colossians 2:17 and Hebrews 10:1 tells us that God established this way to approach Him as shadows of the real Tabernacle, the real sacrifice and the real High Priest who would come later. Then when the "real thing" came along, *there would be no more need to bring animals to a building to be offered by a priest, because the ultimate sacrifice will have been made, all believers would be priests, the Temple would be in us and the laws would be written on our hearts.*

What God established in the Old Covenant was a temporary, preliminary system pointing the Hebrew in the direction of the New Covenant so that they would recognize that "Seed of Abraham" when He came on the scene. In this chapter, we're going to learn how the Tabernacle pointed the Hebrew in that direction. The earthly Tabernacle symbolically represents and points to the real Tabernacle who is Jesus our Lord. *God gave the Tabernacle and the details of its construction to portray in a temporal way, what He would one day do permanently through Jesus.* We are going to discover that the Tabernacle is a visible picture, or model, showing us how we come to God through Jesus. From the foundations of the world, there's only been one way. Jesus is the way.

The Old Covenant

In Exodus 25:1-9, God gives the following instructions to Moses:

> *Jehovah said to Moses, Tell the people of Israel that everyone who wants to may bring me an offering from this list: Gold, silver, bronze, blue cloth, purple cloth, scarlet cloth, fine-twined linen, goat's hair, red-dyed ram's skins, goat-skins, acacia wood, olive oil for the lamps, spices for the anointing oil and for the fragrant incense, onyx stones, stones to be set in the ephod and in the breastplate. For I want the people of Israel to make me a sacred Temple where I can live among them. This home of mine shall be a tent pavilion—a Tabernacle. I will give you a drawing of the construction plan, and the details of each furnishing* (TLB).

The Tabernacle is to be the place where God will meet and dwell with His covenant people. God gives Moses detailed instructions on how to build the Tabernacle in Exodus 25-27. Exodus 35-38 describes its construction. Now the reason God gave such detailed instructions is because this earthly Tabernacle is to foreshadow and be patterned after the real Tabernacle which was then in heaven. (see Hebrews 8:5.) Nothing could be left to chance or man's imagination.

The Earthly Tabernacle

The Tabernacle was the place where the Hebrews would bring their sacrifices for sin and sacrifices of praise. They could only do this at the Tabernacle. They couldn't make sacrifices out in the hills or just anywhere they wanted. *They had to approach God this one way through the Tabernacle.* The Hebrew had to come to the Tabernacle to get to God. He couldn't approach God his own way.

The Tabernacle was portable so that the Hebrews could carry it with them on their journey. Later, when they got into their promised land, a more permanent structure was needed. God then used King Solomon to build a Temple. (see 1 Kings 5-8.) Solomon's Temple was destroyed in 587 B.C. when Jerusalem finally fell to the Babylonians. (see 2 Kings 25:8-9.)

When they returned to their land from Babylon captivity, they rebuilt their Temple. This was in 536 B.C. (see Ezra 1:1-2). However, because of meager resources, this Temple was not as glorious as Solomon's Temple. When the foundations were laid, the old men who had seen Solomon's Temple "wept for sorrow" (Haggai 2:3). About 19 B.C. Herod began to restore this Temple making it more grand and majestic. In A.D. 70 the Temple was destroyed. The Bible tells us the Jews will rebuild the Temple in the latter days just before the return of Jesus. (see Revelation 11:1; Daniel 9:27.) The stage is being set in Israel today for this to happen. It may be sooner than we think.

The Campsite (Numbers 2:2-3)

For this discussion, refer to the drawing titled "Tabernacle in Hebrew Camp," which is at the end of this chapter. Notices that the tribes camped around the Tabernacle are in *specific locations* that God assigned to each of them. Also, each tribe flew its own flag. Speaking to Moses and Aaron, God says, "Each tribe will have its own tent area, with its flagpole and tribal banner; and at the center of these tribal compounds will be the Tabernacle" (Num. 2:2 TLB). Then God assigns the tribal locations as recorded in the rest of Numbers 2 and in Numbers 3.

On the eastern side was the tribe of Judah. The flag for the tribe of Judah was a lion of gold on a field of scarlet. The western tribe was Ephraim. Its flag was a black ox on a field of gold. The southern tribe was Reuben. Reuben's flag was a man on a field of gold. Then on the north side was the tribe of Dan. Its flag was a golden eagle on a field of blue.

The four symbols are referenced again in Ezekiel 1:10 and Revelation 4:7. The lion represents the king that reigns supreme. The ox represents the lowly servant. The man represents the highest earthly being. The eagle represents the greatest heavenly being. We will see the significance of this later.

Clustered around the Tabernacle itself were the *Levite tents*. The Levites were chosen by God to perform sacred duties at the Tabernacle on behalf of the people. The Levite tents surrounded the Tabernacle shielding the people from the wrath of God.

The Courtyard (Exodus 27:9-18; 38:9-20)

The Tabernacle stood inside an outer enclosure or courtyard. The size of this courtyard was 150 feet long and 75 feet wide. That's one-half the length of a football field, and about as wide. Now anyone could go inside the courtyard but only the priest could go inside the Tabernacle itself.

There was yet a further restriction. Only the High Priest could enter the inner room called the Holy of Holies and he could only do this on one day of the year. We will learn more about this is later chapters.

The Coverings (Exodus 26:14)

The Tabernacle had two coverings. The outer covering visible to the passerby was made of badger's skin. It was a dull, unattractive greyish color. *The outsider wouldn't know about the majesty and glory inside the Tabernacle unless he entered in.* The other covering was directly underneath the badger's skin and not visible to the outside passerby. It was made of ram's skin that had been dyed red. Remember the ram was the substitutionary sacrifice for Isaac. And of course, in the Bible, red represents blood. There were also curtains made of linen and goats' hair.

There is much we could say about the courtyard, the fence, the framework, and construction of the Tabernacle. It is a rich study in itself and all points to the greater Tabernacle made without hands. But what I want us to see is how to get into the inner room called the Holy of Holies. This is where God dwells. *Our objective is to get to God.*

For the rest of the chapter, we will be referring to the Tabernacle drawing titled "The Way To God," which is at the end of this chapter. Put yourself in the role of a Hebrew as he/she seeks to approach God through the Tabernacle.

Entrance Gate (Exodus 27:16)

First, you will notice there is only *one way* to get into the courtyard. This way is through the eastern opening called the *Gate.* You cannot get to God except you enter through the eastern Gate. This is the only way in. As you approach the Gate, you must have an acceptable sacrifice to get in.

Brazen Altar (Exodus 27:1-8; 38:1-7)

The first object staring you in the face as you enter the court-yard is the *Brazen Altar* (brazen means brass). It is seven and a half feet square and four and a half feet high. *The Altar is the place where you make your sacrifice.* It is called the "Altar of Burnt Offering." (see Exodus 30:28.) Leviticus 1:9 describes the burnt offering as a sweet savor to the Lord.

You cannot be pardoned from sin and blessed by the priest until you come to this Altar with a sacrifice. You can be the most moral Jew in your tribe but you still have to bring the sacrifice. You can have lots of good works but you still have to bring the sacrifice. Remember the Ten Commandments, the people, the Tabernacle, and all its furnishings were sprinkled with blood. *You don't approach God by trying to keep the Ten Commandments but by the blood sacrifice that God has ordained as acceptable to Him.* Apart from the Brazen Altar, you cannot approach God at all.

God summarizes this way to approach Him in Leviticus 17:11. He says, "For the life of the flesh is in the blood: and I have given it to you upon the altar to make an atonement for your souls: for it is the blood that maketh an atonement for your souls" (KJV).

Remember that in the blood covenant, the sacrifice represents you and will take your place on the Altar. And now as you bring your sacrifice to the Altar, you lay (heavily lean) your hands on the head of the animal claiming its death as a sacrifice on your behalf.

Unless you claim the animal as your sin sacrifice, you cannot be accepted and declared clean. Only with the blood at the Brazen Altar can you enter the Tabernacle and get to God. As you press your hand heavily on the animal's head and kill it, the priest, standing there with you, pours out the blood of the animal at the foot of the Altar.

You approach God by faith, believing in your heart, that through the blood covenant, your sins are symbolically being transmitted to this animal. The slain animal becomes your personal sin substitute. Of course, you realize that the blood of an animal cannot take away your sin. But the blood of the animal will cover your sins until God Himself comes to take them away.

Brazen Laver (Exodus 30:17-21: 38:8)

The next object you encounter is the *Brazen Laver*. The Laver is a *wash basin*, perhaps four or five feet high, filled with water. It is made of polished brass that the women used as a looking glass or mirror.

When Aaron and his sons were consecrated, or set apart as priests, they washed their entire body in the Laver (see Exod. 29:4; Lev. 8:6). This was a ceremonial cleansing. Thereafter, they only had to wash their hands and feet. God required them to wash their hands and feet before entering the Tabernacle and before ministering at the Altar (see Exod. 30:20).

Now as the priest ministered during the day, he would get dirty. So he would come to the Laver and wash. As he looked into the Laver, he would see himself in the polished brass. The Laver showed him how dirty he was and where he needed to wash. But at the same time it showed him how dirty he was, it also provided the water for his cleansing. *Thus, the Laver not only showed him he was dirty, it also cleansed him.*

You cannot enter the Tabernacle unless you have a blood sacrifice and be washed clean in the Laver. You have to come to God by way of the blood and water. We see from the altar and laver that the Outer Courtyard was a picture of salvation.

Holy Place (Exodus 25:30-40; 37:10-28)

You now approach the door of the Tabernacle. It is a linen veil of blue, purple and scarlet. Behind it are hidden the truths of God. Once inside, you see another veil that divides the Tabernacle into two rooms...the Holy Place and the Holy of Holies. The first outer room is called the Holy Place. The Holy of Holies is the inner room behind the veil. Behind this veil dwells the presence of God. You are trying to get into this inner room. But first you must pass through the Holy Place. There are three pieces of furnishings in the Holy Place; the *Golden Candlestick*, the *Table of Shewbread*, and the *Incense Altar.*

Golden Candlestick (Exodus 25:31-39; 27:20-21; 37:17-24)

Immediately to your left is the *Golden Candlestick.* It weighs about 107 pounds and has seven branches. *The middle branch is the central shaft that continually feeds oil to the other six branches.* These six branches, in turn, illuminate the taller central shaft. They are trimmed morning and evening to insure continuous light. The Golden Candlestick provides all the light for the Holy Place. No natural light can get in.

Table of Shewbread (Exodus 25:23-30; 37:10-16)

To your right, directly across from the Golden Candlestick, is the *Table of Shewbread.* This table is three feet long, one and a half feet wide, and two and a half feet high.

Twelve loaves of bread (one loaf for each of the 12 tribes) are placed on the table in two heaps of six loaves. Then the loaves are covered with frankincense. Every Sabbath the old loaves are removed and eaten by the priest and new loaves are placed on the table. On the table beside the loaves are trays and vessels of wine.

The Table of Shewbread, with the accompanying bread and wine, represents the blood covenant meal. The covenant is cut at the Brazen Altar. The animal that was sacrificed represents the person entering into covenant. But instead of eating the animal and drinking its blood; bread and wine is offered. For six days the bread and wine sets on the table. It represents the life (body and blood) of the person being offered to God. In this case, the 12 loaves represent the entire nation in covenant with God. On the Sabbath, the priest eats the bread and pours out the wine symbolically feeding on and receiving into himself (and the people he represents) the life of God.

Altar of Incense (Exodus 37:25-28)

Straight ahead of you and directly in front of the second veil is the *Altar of Incense.* The Altar is three feet high and one and a half feet square. Every morning and evening the priest puts burning coals on this Altar. He then sprinkles incense over the coals. When the incense touches the coals, it fills the room with a fragrant white cloud of smoke. Once a year, on the Day of Atonement, the priest sprinkles blood from the sin offering on the horns of this Altar and enters the Holy of Holies with incense billowing up in front of him.

While the Outer Courtyard was a picture of salvation, the Holy Place is a picture of service. The lampstand, table of showbread and alter of incense are pictures of priestly service and our ministry to God and people.

Holy of Holies

The second veil separates the Holy of Holies from the Holy Place. This veil was so woven together that two pairs of oxen attached to either side and driven in opposite directions could not tear it apart. *Behind this veil is the throne room of God. This is your destination.* But your way is blocked. You can't go behind the veil. You can't enter into God's presence. Only the High Priest can enter God's presence and he only on the Day of Atonement.

Ark of the Covenant (Exodus 25:10-22; 37:1-9)

The only piece of furniture in the Holy of Holies is the *Ark of the Covenant.* The Ark of the Covenant is a small chest 3 3/4 feet long, 2 1/4 feet wide and 2 1/4 feet high. The lid attached to the Ark is called *"The Mercy Seat."*

The Greek word that means the same as the Hebrew word for Mercy Seat is *hilasterion.* The English word for hilasterion is "propitiation." *Propitiation simply means to make a way to be reconciled to God by satisfying His holy justice which requires sin to be dealt with.* Remember the only offering that will satisfy His justice is blood because the penalty or judgment of sin is death. It is the only evidence that the penalty for sin has been paid. *The Mercy Seat is the place of propitiation.* This is where the blood will be applied.

God is not a blood thirsty deity who delights in seeing things die. He wants us to have life. It is our sin that demands death and blood is the evidence the judgment has been paid.

A replica of a cherubim (angel) is attached to each end of the Mercy Seat. Their wings are outstretched touching each other at the middle of the lid.

Right between the two cherubim and above the Mercy Seat is a blinding light. This bright light is called the *Shekinah,* meaning the presence of God's glory. It is the manifested presence of God dwelling in the midst of the people. *The Holy of Holies is God's earthly throne room, the Mercy Seat is His throne and the great light is His visible presence.* (See Psalm 99:1)

Three objects were placed inside the Ark under the Mercy Seat. These were Aaron's rod that budded with almonds, a small pot of manna and the stone tablets containing the Ten Commandments (Heb. 9:4).

Aaron's rod reminded God that the Hebrews had earlier rejected His leadership through Aaron (Num. 16-17). The pot of manna spoke of the Hebrews earlier rejection of God's earthly provisions (Num. 11). The Ten Commandments were broken by the Hebrews and reminded God that the people fall short of His holiness and glory (Exod. 32).

Every day God would look down from His cloud of glory and see man's evidence of sin. And the penalty for sin is death. God's justice must be administered. He cannot allow rebellion. His wrath must be vindicated.

But on the Day of Atonement, the High Priest comes behind the veil into the Holy of Holies with the blood of the innocent sacrifice. This is the sacrifice God has ordained to take your place in the blood covenant until He comes Himself on your behalf.

As incense fills the room, the High Priest sprinkles the blood of the sacrifice over the Mercy Seat. At that moment, as God looks down from His cloud of glory, He doesn't see the evidence of man's sin. Instead He sees the blood. The blood of the innocent sacrifice tells God that life has been given to pay the penalty. *The blood-covered Mercy Seat (not the Ten Commandments) changes God's throne from one of judgment to one of mercy.* Justice has been administered. God has made a way for sinners to be reconciled to Him.

While the Outer Courtyard represents salvation and the Holy Place represents service, the Holy of Holies represents worship where we can stand forgiven in the presence of God. As we will discover, these three areas of the Tabernacle picture the Messiah and three phases in our walk with God through salvation, service, and worship.

The New Covenant

The Campsite

The flags of each tribe point us to the real banner of God, Jesus our Lord, as He is portrayed in the four gospels. In Matthew, Jesus is presented as the King of the Jews (the lion from the tribe of Judah). In Mark, He is the suffering servant (the ox). In Luke, He is the Son of Man. In John, Jesus is revealed as the Son of God (the greatest heavenly being).

As the Son of God, Jesus represents God to man. As the Son of Man, He represents man to God. Like the Levite, He stands between God and man shielding man from the judgment of God by His blood.

The Coverings

John 1:1 says, "In the beginning was the Word, and the Word was with God and the Word was God" (KJV). John continues this statement in verse 14 and says, "And the Word was made flesh and dwelt among us, and we beheld his glory, the glory as of the only begotten of the Father full of grace and truth" (John 1:14 KJV).

The word that became flesh and dwelt among us is Jesus of Nazareth. (see John 1:15; Revelation 19:13.) The Greek word for dwelt is *skenoo*. It means to encamp, occupy, reside, indwell, or "tabernacle." God would tabernacle among us in the human person of Jesus. In Him dwelled all the fullness of the Godhead bodily (see Col. 1:19; 2:9).

God's glory had dwelled in the Holy of Holies in the earthly Tabernacle and Temple made with hands; now it was to dwell in the flesh of Jesus, the heavenly Tabernacle made without hands. Jesus was made without hands in that He was begotten of God, not man. He was born of a virgin. It was His body that God prepared for Himself. (see Hebrews 2:14; 10:5.)

John beheld His glory, the glory as of the only begotten of the Father. Paul writes in Second Corinthians 4:6 that the glory of God shines in the face of Jesus. Paul even referred to Jesus as "the Lord of Glory" (1 Cor. 2:8).

Hebrews 1:1-3 puts it this way: "In many and various ways God spoke of old to our fathers by the prophets; but in these last days he has spoken to us by a Son, whom He appointed..." (RSV).

But like the badger's skin veiled God's glory in the earthly Tabernacle, it was also veiled in Jesus (see Phil. 2:7). *To the passerby, there was nothing exciting about this carpenter from Nazareth.* Why, He looked just like everybody else. The casual observer standing on the outside wouldn't know the Lord of Glory was dwelling among them.

But as the ram's skin that had been dyed red, *the blood of God flowed underneath the outer shell of Jesus' body.* It was to be the substitutionary blood to take away the sins of all who would enter into covenant with Him. He was that seed of Abraham.

Through the blood covenant, He would come to live in us by His spirit. We then would become the Tabernacle or dwelling place of God. After Jesus was resurrected, He appeared to His disciples to show them He was victorious over death. On one of those occasions He breathed on them and said, "...Receive the Holy Spirit" (John 20:22 NIV).

Now that Jesus has sent the Holy Spirit, the believer's body is the dwelling place of God. *He no longer dwells in a tent in the desert, or brick and mortar on some street corner. He dwells in all who have entered into blood covenant with Him and received His Spirit.* The individual believer is the temple of the Holy Spirit. The Lord of Glory has come to take up residence in all of His creation who will ask him to come into their heart. (see 1 Corinthians 3:16; 6:19-20; 2 Corinthians 6:16; Ephesians 1:14; 2:21-22.)

Yet to the passerby, there is nothing exciting about being a Christian. It appears to be a very unattractive, dull and boring life. Their attitude is, "Who wants to be a Christian? Why you have got to have a long face and never have any fun." They don't know that all the riches of God's inheritance dwells in His people (Eph. 1:11). The only way they'll find out is by coming into this perfect Tabernacle of God, Jesus, the human, now exalted, Lord of Glory. They must become "in Him" to experience the glory of God.

The Gate

The Gate into the Tabernacle was on the eastern side. The tribe of Judah camped in front of the Gate. Remember its flag was a lion of gold on a field of scarlet. Speaking of the Temple that was later constructed, Ezekiel says, "And the glory of the LORD came into the house by the way of the gate whose prospect is toward the east" (Ezek. 43:4 KJV). The Hebrew had to come through this Gate to get to God. There was no other way.

Jesus' lineage is of the tribe of Judah. Gold represents deity. The lion is the king that reigns supreme; yet he's covered by a field of scarlet blood. Revelation 5:5 says, "Jesus is the Lion from the tribe of Judah." The tribe of Judah, its flag, and the Eastern Gate all pointed the Hebrew to Jesus who said, "...I am the way—and the truth and the life. No one comes to the Father except through me" (John 14:6 NIV).

The Altar

For the believer, the Courtyard represents the place of salvation. *The Brazen Altar is the cross of Jesus.* This is where the new covenant was cut. As the blood was poured out at the base of the Altar, the blood of Jesus was poured out at the foot of the cross. He gave Himself for us an offering and a sacrifice to God for a sweet smelling savor (see Eph. 5:2).

On one appearance to His disciples after His resurrection, Jesus said, "...Why are you troubled and why do questions rise in your hearts? See my hands and my feet, that it is I myself; handle me, and see; for a spirit has not flesh and bones as you see that I have" (Luke 24:38-39 RSV). Now we would have said flesh and blood. But Jesus said flesh and bones because He gave His blood for us.

Unfortunately, we have all sinned and come short of the glory of God (Rom. 3:23). A thick veil blocks our way and keeps us from coming into the Holy of Holies where God dwells. And the penalty for our sin is death. *Being the best moral person in the community won't help us. Good works won't save us. The Ten Commandments can't bring us into God's presence. They only condemn us because we can't keep them.* The life of the flesh is in the blood and without the shedding of blood there is no forgiveness of sin (see Lev. 17:11; Heb. 9:22).

All our self-righteousness is like filthy rags to God (see Isa. 64:6). We may be good compared to our neighbor, but our neighbor is not the standard God uses. He compares us to Himself and not one of us can measure up to His perfect, absolute standards. We cannot approach God with our own goodness.

But Jesus, who knew no sin, became sin for us that we might be the righteousness of God in Him (see 2 Cor. 5:21). We approach God, not with our own righteousness but through faith in Jesus (see Phil. 3:9).

When we personally accept by faith the blood of Jesus as our own substitutionary sacrifice for sin, His righteousness is imputed or counted to us. *We then can enter into that more perfect Tabernacle in heaven, right into the heavenly Holy of Holies based on what Jesus did for us, not on what we try to do for God.*

But where the blood of bulls and goats in the Old Covenant only covered sin, the blood of Jesus takes it away to be remembered no more. No more sacrifices are needed, for the once and for all sacrifice has been made (see Heb. 9-10). This is what Jesus meant when He cried from the cross, "It is finished." (See John 20:30.) The sin debt has been "paid in full" for all who receive it for themselves.

All who will come to the cross of Jesus are to offer themselves to God as a living sacrifice (see Rom. 12:1). We become His purchased possession paid for by His own blood. Out of love to our divine covenant partner we, who claim the name "Christian" are to glorify God in our body and spirit, which belong to God. (see 1 Corinthians 3:16; 6:19-20; 2 Corinthians 6:16; Ephesians 1:14; 2:21-22.) Because of His great grace to enter into covenant with us, we give Him our worship, our praise, our thanksgiving, our life.

The Laver

Whereas the Altar points to the death of Jesus, *the Laver points to His life coming into us through the Holy Spirit.* One night a Jewish religious leader named Nicodemus came to Jesus and inquired of Him…"Rabbi, we know that thou art a teacher come from God: for no man can do these miracles that thou doest, except God be with him" (John 3:2 KJV).

Jesus replied, "...verily, verily, I say unto thee, except a man be born again, he cannot see the kingdom of God" (John 3:3 KJV).

Nicodemus didn't understand what Jesus meant. So he asked, "...How can a man be born when he is old? Can he enter the second time into his mother's womb, and be born?" (John 3:4 KJV).

Jesus replied, "...Verily, verily, I say unto thee, except a man be born of water and the spirit, he cannot enter into the kingdom of God. That which is born of the flesh is flesh; and that which is born of the spirit is spirit. Marvel not that I said unto thee, ye must be born again" John 3:5-7 KJV).

Later Jesus met a Samaritan woman at Jacob's well. Pointing to the well He told her that, "...Everyone who drinks this water will be thirsty again, but whoever drinks the water I give him will never thirst. Indeed, the water I give him will become in him a spring of water welling up to everlasting life" (John 4:13-14 NIV).

At the Feast of Tabernacles, when water from the pool of Siloam was being poured into a basin at the foot of the Altar, Jesus stood and proclaimed,

> ...If any one thirst, let him come to me and drink. He who believes in me, as the Scripture has said, 'Out of his heart shall flow rivers of living water.' Now this he said about the Spirit, which those who believed in him were to receive; for as yet the Spirit had not been given, because Jesus was not yet glorified (John 7:38-39 RSV).

Paul writes that we receive the life of God through blood covenant, "not because of righteous works that we have done but in agreement with His mercy, He saved us through the washing of regeneration and a renewing of the Holy Spirit, whom He has poured out richly on us through Jesus Christ our Savior, so that counted as righteous by His grace, we might be made heirs in accordance with our hope of eternal life" (Titus 3:5-7 TLB).

The word for regeneration in Greek is *paliggenesia*. It means to have a *spiritual rebirth*. God spoke of this spiritual cleansing through the Old Covenant prophet Ezekiel. He said,

> *Then will I sprinkle clean water upon you, and ye shall be clean; from all your filthiness and from all your idols, will I cleanse you. A new heart also will I give you and a new spirit will I put within you: and I will take away the stony heart out of your flesh; and I will give you an heart of flesh. And I will put my spirit within you and cause you to walk in my statutes, and ye shall keep my judgments* (laws) *and do them. And ye shall dwell in the land that I gave to your fathers; and ye shall be my people and I will be your God* (Ezekiel 36:25-28 KJV).

His Blood Is Enough

When we accept Jesus as our Savior and Lord, His blood cleanses us from all our sins, past, present and future (1 John 1:7). His righteousness is imputed or counted to us. (see Romans 4:22-24; 2 Corinthians 5:21; Philippians 3:9; Romans 8:4.) We approach God on the merit of His Son. We are set aside to be ministering priests of the Most High God. And we never have to go back to the Brazen Altar again. We never have to go back to the cross to be born again "again." While we certainly need to go to the cross to repent of our sins, His blood is enough to cover all our failures and reconcile us to our God.

Christians are people who have been given supernatural faith by the Holy Spirit to believe in their own human spirit (not head) that Jesus died for their sins. When people receive that faith from God and claim Jesus as their personal Savior, confessing with their mouth what they already believe in their spirit (heart) the Holy Spirit comes to live in them (see Rom. 10:9-10).

When a person believes, he enters into blood covenant with God through the Lord Jesus. The blood covenant is an everlasting covenant. *Staying in the covenant depends on God's grace and mercy, not our good works.* Of course this assumes we were truly in the covenant in the first place as manifested by the Fruit of the Spirit. This is sometimes hard for us to understand because our modern salvation experience often falls far short of a blood covenant commitment. If we are truly a "born-again" believer, it will be evidenced by Holy Spirit inspired works of covenantal love manifested in our lives. Even though we may often fail God in our attitudes and actions, our love for God motivates us to want to please Him. His love for us offers forgiveness.

A biblical blood covenant is much more than simply an agreement to be friends. It is a commitment of our life to another person, in this instance, Jesus our Lord. This relationship is not the same as the casual Western "once saved always saved" salvation that is often very shallow and based on emotions rather than commitment.

Of course we can walk away from this relationship and turn our back on God. But if we truly want God in our lives, we have a sacred blood covenant relationship that God Himself guarantees. While our spirit is saved when we are born again, our soul is constantly "being saved" as the Holy Spirit redeems our mind, emotions, and will. Theologically speaking, we were saved in our spirit (past), we are being saved in our soul (present), and we will be saved in our body (future). Hallelujah!

Christianity is not a religion; it is a relationship with Almighty God through His Son. The Holy Spirit joins us in a spiritual union with God and confirms this to our heart. He is in us and we are in Him.

When a person receives the Holy Spirit, the Holy Spirit seals that person in the covenant. (see Ephesians 1:13; 4:30; 2 Corinthians 1:22; 1 Peter 1:3-5; Jude 24.) The Holy Spirit then testifies or bears witness to our own human spirit that we are in blood covenant and a child of God (see Rom. 8:15-17). While we can grieve the Holy Spirit by the way we live our lives (Eph. 4:30), God promises that He will never leave us nor forsake us (Heb. 13:5).

Fellowship Not Fathership

Although the blood covenant position of a true believer with God cannot be broken, our fellowship with Him can. As we walk in the world ministering as a priest of God, we get dirty spiritually...we sin. This sin breaks our fellowship with God. Instead of going back to the Altar to be born again and again and again and again, we go to the Laver. When we go to the Laver, we don't have to be washed all over again. We only have to wash our hands and feet, which represents our service to God and our walk with God—that part of our soul that needs to be sanctified. This means that our soul need to be saved or renewed every day.

The water in the Laver points us to the Holy Spirit. The polished brass mirror points to the word of God as revealed through the Bible.

The Holy Spirit uses the Bible to wash us clean. (see John 17:17; Ephesians 5:26.) When we look into the Bible, it is like looking into a mirror. The Bible is God's holy looking glass that reveals our sin.

At the same time, the Bible is also like a tub of hot water that the Holy Spirit uses to cleanse us, as we allow Him to. The Holy Spirit scrubs us down real good with the Word of God wherever we're dirty. After this spiritual bath, we are a lot cleaner than we were beforehand.

The same Word of God that reveals our sins also washes them away by the power of the Holy Spirit. This washing of our hands and feet by the Holy Spirit restores our fellowship with God so that we, like the Old Covenant priest, can go into His presence and minister on His behalf.

The Holy Place

Now that we have come by way of the blood and the water, we can now enter through the Door of the Tabernacle. Jesus said in John 10:9, "I am the door; if anyone enters by me, he will be saved, and will go in and out and find pasture" (RSV). For the believer, the Holy Place represents the place of service.

The Golden Candlestick

The Golden Candlestick points us to the three personal expressions of God: the Father, the Son, and the Holy Spirit. First John 1:5 says, "...God is light, and in Him is no darkness at all" (KJV). In John 9:5, Jesus says, "As long as I am in the world, I am the light of the world" (KJV). Yet on another occasion, Jesus speaking to all who would receive Him said, "You are the light of the world" (Matt. 5:14 RSV).

Now how can this be? How can God be the light, Jesus be the light, and believers be the light? There's only one way.

Jesus explained it when He spoke of the time He would send the Holy Spirit to indwell believers. He said, "In that day you will know that I am in my Father, and you in me, and I in you" (John 14:20 RSV). Believers have received the light of life in them in the person of the Holy Spirit.

Since the Father, the Son, and the Holy Spirit all claim to be the light; they all have to be personal expressions of the One True God. We, in turn, are light bearers.

This is most clearly taught in the Golden Candlestick. Gold represents deity. The Candlestick itself represents the Father. The central shaft points us to the Son, Jesus Christ. The oil symbolizes the Holy Spirit. The six branches fed by the Holy Spirit represent believers.

While writing the book of Revelation, John heard behind him a great voice. When he turned to see who was speaking, he said, "...I saw seven golden candlesticks; and in the midst of the seven golden candlesticks one like unto the Son of Man, clothed with a garment down to the foot, and girt about the paps with a golden girdle" (Revelation 1:12-13 KJV).

John saw Jesus standing in the midst of the Candlestick wearing His High Priestly clothing as He intercedes for the Church. As the central shaft fed oil to the six branches, the branches not only gave off light but also illuminated the central shaft. Likewise, Jesus has sent the Holy Spirit to indwell all believers. The Holy Spirit is our power source. Through His life flowing in us, we not only give off light; but we also illuminate (draw attention to) Jesus.

The Candlestick provided the only light in the Tabernacle. No natural light could get in. This points to the believer walking in the power of the Holy Spirit (being fed by the oil) rather than trying to serve Jesus in the energy of the flesh. We cannot give off light nor glorify Jesus by trying to serve God through our own natural abilities.

Striving to keep the Ten Commandments, or a list of do's and don'ts, only leads to failure, frustration and defeat. It will never glorify our Lord. That is the work of the Holy Spirit. It is His light that is to shine before men. When His light is shining, others will see His good works in our life and God will be glorified. (see Matthew 5:16.)

By good works, Jesus does not mean "being active in all the programs at the church." He means that His own character of holiness and righteousness is to be manifested through us by the power of the Holy Spirit. (see John 15:26; 16:14; Ephesians 1:4; 2:10; Galatians 5:22-25.)

As the branches were trimmed morning and evening to insure continuous light, the believer must continuously be filled with the Holy Spirit in order to radiate the light of life in him (see Eph. 5:18). If you have this need in your own life, ask God to fill you with His Spirit so you can live a life that glorifies Him.

The Table of Shewbread

The blood covenant meal at the Table of Shewbread, points to the time when man would have communion with God through the Holy Spirit. In John 6, Jesus presents Himself as the Bread of Life. He explained it this way:

> *...I am the living bread that came down from heaven. If a man eats of this bread, he will live forever. This bread is my flesh, which I will give for the life of the*

world. Then the Jews began to argue sharply among themselves, How can this man give us his flesh to eat?

Jesus said to them, I tell you the truth, unless you eat the flesh of the Son of Man and drink His blood, you have no life in you. Whoever eats my flesh and drinks my blood has eternal life, and I will raise him up at the last day. For my flesh is real food and my blood is real drink. Whoever eats my flesh and drinks my blood remains in me, and I in him. Just as the living Father sent me and I live because of the Father, so the one who feeds on me will live because of me. This is the bread that came down from heaven. Our forefathers ate manna and died; but he who feeds on this bread will live forever (John 6:51-58 NIV).

In John 6:55, Jesus claims to be the "real thing" who has now come to be the spiritual reality of the Old Covenant through His blood sacrifice. Jesus, seeing that the people didn't understand what He was talking about, further explained Himself. In John 6:63, He says, "...the words that I have spoken to you are spirit and life" (RSV). Divine-Human union is of the spirit; not of the flesh.

The Altar of Incense

The blood sprinkled horns of the Incense Altar were proof that the sin offering had been made. This blood evidence allowed the High Priest to enter the Holy of Holies into the presence of God. As he went behind the Veil, the incense billowed up in front of the Ark of the Covenant and the manifested presence of God in the glory cloud.

But he could only go in once a year. And the Veil hid God's presence so that no one else could approach Him. This was because the sacrifice was incomplete and had to be offered year after year. The blood of bulls and goats only covered the people's sins; it didn't take them away.

Incense is a symbol of prayer (see Ps. 141:2). It represents the high priestly prayers of Jesus and our prayer offered in His name. (see John 17:9-10; Revelation 5:8; 8:3-4.) Jesus is worthy to petition to the Father on our behalf because His own blood is on the Incense Altar. Through His blood, God receives our prayers offered in the name of Jesus.

The Holy of Holies

The Veil that hid "the glory" represented the veiled glory of God in the *human body of Jesus.* When Jesus was crucified, His Father in heaven split the Veil from top to bottom. (see Matthew 27:51; Mark 15:38; Luke 23:45.) It was no longer needed because the once and for all perfect sacrifice was being made. Whereas, the blood of bulls and goats only covered sins, the blood of Jesus takes them away. No more sacrifices are needed.

The blood of Jesus opens the way for all to go right into the heavenly throne room of God and commune with Him through the Holy Spirit. (see Ephesians 2:13-18; Colossians 1:20-22; Hebrews 10:1-22.) So for the believer, the Holy of Holies represents the place of worship and intimacy.

Earlier we read about a Samaritan woman who met Jesus at Jacob's well. Samaritans were part Jew and part Gentile. They worshiped God on Mount Gerizim which was north of Jerusalem. The Jews, including Jesus, worshiped God in Jerusalem. Jesus revealed some facts about the woman's past that He would not have known without divine knowledge. This prompted the following conversation recorded in John 4:19-24.

The woman saith unto him, Sir, I perceive that thou art a prophet. Our fathers worshiped in this mountain; and ye say, that in Jerusalem is the place where men ought to worship. Jesus saith unto her, Woman believe me, the hour cometh, when ye shall neither in this mountain, nor yet at Jerusalem, worship the Father. Ye worship ye know not what: we know what we worship: for salvation is of the Jews. But the hour cometh, and now is, when the true worshipers shall worship the Father in spirit and in truth: for the Father seeketh such to worship him. God is a Spirit: and they that worship him must worship him in Spirit and in truth (John 4:19-24 KJV).

Jesus was saying the day was soon coming when a person wouldn't have to "go somewhere" to worship God. We would be able to worship God out of our own spirit in communion with the Holy Spirit. The Holy Spirit would take us right into "Father's house" (the heavenly Holy of Holies) regardless of where we might be physically. In other words, we wouldn't go to church, we would be the church, the people of God, by our receiving the Holy Spirit.

Much that goes under the name of worship is not really worship but merely a satisfying of man's religious obligations and soothing of his seared conscience. *The only true worship is in "Father's house."* All who desire true worship may go there because the Veil has been removed.

The Ark of the Covenant

Jesus as the perfect sacrifice ascended into the heavenly Holy of Holies to sprinkle His own blood over the Ark of the Covenant in God's heavenly throne room. When he offered it, He sat down on the throne.

Remember the blood-covered Mercy Seat was attached to the top of the Ark of the Covenant. It was the place of propitiation. Likewise, Jesus is on the throne of God (see Acts 2:30; Rev. 3:21; 21:5). The slain but resurrected "Lamb of God" is on the throne (see Rev. 5:6-9).

Jesus was the perfect One who fulfilled in Himself Aaron's rod that budded, the pot of manna, and the stone tablets. He did this by being our perfect High Priest, the Unleavened Bread of God from Heaven and by perfectly keeping the Law of God. Therefore, it is His blood that completely satisfies God's judgment on sin. It is His blood that changes God's throne from one of judgment to one of mercy. (see Hebrews 4:14-16; 9:6-15.)

> *Therefore by the deeds of the law there shall no flesh be justified [declared not guilty] in his sight: for by the law is the knowledge of sin* [the law shows us we are sinners]. *But now the righteousness of God without the law is manifested, being witnessed by the law and the prophets; even the righteousness of God which is by faith of [in] Jesus Christ* [Messiah] *unto all and upon all them that believe: for there is no difference:*
>
> *For all have sinned and come short of the glory of God; Being justified freely by His grace,* (not our merit) *through the redemption* [purchasing our salvation] *that is in Christ* [Messiah] *Jesus: Whom God set forth to be a propitiation through faith in His blood* [not the Ten Commandments]*, to declare his righteousness for the remission of sins that are past, through the forbearance of God;* (Romans 3:20-25 RSV).

...And if any man sin, we have an advocate with the Father, Jesus Christ [Messiah] *the righteous: And he is the propitiation for our sins: and not for ours only, but also for the sins of the whole world* (1 John 2:1-2).

The Covenant Is Eternal

The blood covenant is an eternal, everlasting covenant. All who enter into it will dwell with God forever. The apostle John puts it this way in Revelation 21:1-7:

And I saw a new heaven and a new earth; for the first heaven and the first earth were passed away: and there was no more sea. And I, John, saw the holy city, New Jerusalem, coming down from God out of heaven, prepared as a bride adorned for her husband. And 1 heard a great voice out of heaven saying, Behold, the tabernacle of God is with men, and he will dwell with them, and they shall be his people, and God himself shall be with them, and be their God. And God shall wipe away all tears from their eyes; and there shall be no more death, neither sorrow, nor crying, neither shall there be any more pain: for the former things are passed away.

And he that sat upon the throne said, Behold, I make all things new. And he said unto me, Write: for these words are true and faithful. And he said unto me, It is done. I am Alpha and Omega, the beginning and the end. I will give unto him that is athirst of the fountain of the water of life freely. He that overcometh shall inherit all things; and I will be his God, and he shall be my son (Revelation 21:7 KJV).

If you've been trying to approach God through the Ten Commandments, you now see how hopeless that is. God's absolute standards are beyond your reach. Even when you are at your best, you simply cannot measure up to His perfect holiness. Like the Hebrew of old, you too must flee to the real Tabernacle of God, Jesus, the Messiah of the Jews and Savior of the Gentiles. He is waiting for you. Make that commitment now and your life will change forever.

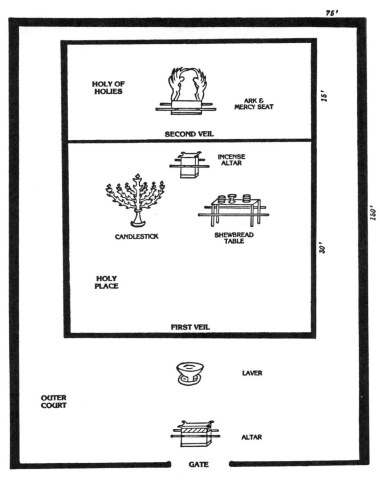

WAY TO GOD

Chapter 5

THE SACRIFICES

Review

When God appeared to the Hebrews to give them the law, it was an awesome sight. There were tremendous thunder and lightning storms. Mount Sinai was covered with smoke that billowed into the sky like a furnace. The whole mountain shook with a violent earthquake. And God commanded the people not even to come near the mountain, "lest they die."

You see, He is a holy God and He was about to reveal Himself to His covenant people. Already they had been murmuring and complaining. Yet the parties to a covenant cannot walk together unless they are in agreement. Well, it was quite evident the Hebrews didn't know much about their covenant partner.

So God said, "It's about time I introduce myself to you. It's about time you meet your covenant provider." So He booms out the Ten Commandments. Through the Ten Commandments and the other laws accompanying them, God was saying, "This is what I am like. This is my character. This is who you are in covenant with."

Along with the laws, we've learned that God also gave instructions for building the Tabernacle, for ordaining the priesthood, and for establishing an elaborate system for making sacrifices.

Then we read that Moses built an altar and offered a sacrifice to God. He took the blood of the sacrificed animals and splashed it against the altar. He also threw blood toward the people themselves. In the same manner, he sprinkled blood over the Book of the Covenant containing the Ten Commandments and accompanying laws. Later he would sprinkle blood over the Tabernacle and all its furnishings used in worship. Then Moses declared before the people, "…This blood confirms and seals the covenant the Lord has made with you in giving you these laws" (Exodus 24:8 TLB). The writer of Hebrews puts it this way:

> *Hence even the first covenant was not ratified without blood. For when every commandment of the law had been declared by Moses to all the people, he took the blood of calves and goats, with water and scarlet wool and hyssop, and sprinkled both the book itself and all the people, saying, 'This is the blood of the covenant*

which God commanded you.' And in the same way he sprinkled with the blood both the tent [Tabernacle] and all the vessels used in worship. Indeed, under the law almost everything is purified with blood, and without the shedding of blood there is no forgiveness of sins (Hebrews 9:18-22 RSV).

We learn from this that God gave the law, not as part of the blood covenant, but as his way of revealing Himself to the world. It was His calling card to show the world His character. In this respect, the law served as God's divine mirror. When the Hebrew looked into the Ten Commandments, he would see God's holiness and his sinfulness.

This would enable the Hebrew to recognize the infinite gap between God and himself. He could understand that he had sinned and fallen short of God's glory and without the shedding of blood there would be no forgiveness of sin. This revelation would drive the Hebrew to the blood covenant as his means of being reconciled to God.

You see, God was showing the world through His covenant people, that we approach Him by His grace and mercy provided through the blood covenant. With the revelation of His absolute divine holiness, we could realize the futility of seeking to reconcile ourselves to God by trying to be a "good person" and keep God's commandments. We would come to understand, that even at our best, we don't measure up to a holy God. We too, then, would run to the blood covenant.

The Tabernacle, priesthood, and sacrifice system were of the Old Covenant. But they pointed the Hebrew to the New Covenant when God, Himself, would come in the flesh. His coming would fulfill His promise to Abraham, which was "...that from

Abraham's seed (singular) would come one who would be a blessing to the whole world." When He came, He would be the reality of these temporary provisions that pointed to Him. The physical pictures would find their fulfillment in the Person of Jesus of Nazareth Who was the perfect Tabernacle of God, the perfect sacrifice and the perfect High Priest.

In the last chapter, we learned that God established a Tabernacle, a sacrifice system, and a priesthood as the way for the Hebrew to approach Him. We saw how the Tabernacle was a physical representation showing us the way to God. We now want to learn about the sacrifices.

Background

In the beginning, God created a perfect universe that was orderly and harmoniously operated within His will. But man chose to rebel against God's will. Man's rebellion brought chaos and destruction on himself and everything around him. We only need to look around to realize this truth.

God calls man's rebellion...*sin*. He says we all do it because it's our nature. It is within us. A lot of people try to blame the devil for their actions. *But God says sin is an inside job.* (see Mark 7:20-23; Ephesians 2:3; James 1:14.)

Now man's sin was no big surprise to God. Adam didn't sneak up on God and pull a fast one while God was napping. God knew all along what would happen when He created man. Of course He would, since He is God.

God didn't cause rebellion, but He allowed it. God allowed it because He loves us enough to give us a free will that He will not violate. God doesn't cause us to sin but He allows us to. He won't force us to love Him. Forced love isn't really love, is it? But God warned Adam that the day he sinned by eating the forbidden fruit he would die. (see Genesis 2:17.) The penalty for sin is death. And what is the evidence that the penalty has been paid? Why, it is blood. Shed blood is the evidence that life has been given to pay the penalty. God had forewarned Adam.

God's Dilemma

Now God is a God of order. He cannot tolerate rebellion in His universe. If He allowed rebellion to go unpunished, He would cease to be God and His universe would fall apart. It would become an uncontrolled, chaotic mess.

We can get a pretty good idea of God's viewpoint by looking at our own country. Failure to apply the law of the land has resulted in disrespect for the law and a lawlessness and chaos that is almost uncontrollable.

Well God can't allow this to happen to Himself nor His universe. So He says rebellion must be punished. But God is also a God of love. He loves us but He must judge us for our rebellion. He cannot exercise His love at the expense of His justice. So He made a provision for dealing with our rebellion. He made this provision before Adam and Eve's rebellion ever took place. *God knew it would happen so He planned ahead on how to deal with it.* That sounds like a God of order, doesn't it?

God's Plan

God's plan says, "Although the penalty for sin is death, you don't have to pay it. I'll come to earth and pay it for you. I'll purchase your salvation with my own blood." This is God's provision.

Wow.

This is the "out" God ordained for us because it satisfies His perfect love without violating His perfect justice.

From the beginning, God determined that He would provide Himself, His own blood, as the evidence that the judgment had been paid. *God determined that at a certain time in history, He would become the "Lamb of God" that takes away the sins of the world.* (see 1 Peter 1:18-20.) All who have believed and accepted God's plan in their heart have been saved from the sin penalty by looking to the time when God would literally come to the earth and cut the covenant by the shedding of His own blood.

God Gives a Preview

God gave us a preview of His plan from the very beginning. He tells us about it in Genesis chapter 3. Here is what happened. When Adam and Eve sinned, they covered themselves with leaves and hid from God. This was *their way* of covering their sin. Well, when God saw Adam and Eve covered with those fig leaves, He knew it was time to explain the "spiritual facts of life."

But how could He do it? How could He explain His plan in terms they could understand? There was only one way. He must kill an innocent animal and accept its blood in substitute as a temporary covering of their sin. It would be an imperfect substitute and only cover sin. But it would point everybody in the right direction. Then when He came along Himself, He would be the perfect substitute. His blood would do more than just cover sin. It would take it away. Then no more sacrifices would be needed.

So God killed an animal and showed it to Adam and Eve. Now Adam and Eve had never seen death before. You and I are accustomed to death. Not so with Adam and Eve. It must have made them sick to see life taken away from one of God's creatures.

Although God didn't have Moses record the details of His plan in this preview account, He certainly must have explained it to Adam and Eve. I believe He had Adam watch Him kill the animal and then said, "Adam, you remember I told you the penalty for sin is death? Well, this is what I'm talking about. Horrible, isn't it? Makes your stomach draw into knots, doesn't it? I don't like it any more than you do, but My righteousness judgment must be administered."

"Now do you understand how horrible sin is in My sight? I can't even stand to look at it. And those fig leaves you are wearing can't hide your sins. Because when I look at you with those fig leaves, I don't see the proper evidence that the price has been paid. I still see your sins and My eyes are too holy to look at you. So your way of covering your sins is not acceptable.

"But if you will accept this dead animal as your sin substitute, I'll let it pay the price for you. I'll let it temporarily cover your sins until I come Myself and take them away."

Then God clothed Adam and Eve with the skins of the innocent animal. At this time, He evidently instructed Adam to bring an acceptable sacrifice and later when children would come along; Adam would teach them to do the same. This was because all of humanity would now inherit Adam's sin nature (see Rom. 5:12; Eph. 2:3). *All would require the innocent substitutionary sacrifice.*

From then on when God saw Adam and Eve clothed with the animal skins, He saw the evidence that the price had been paid. It was a constant reminder to Him forever. God saw them clothed with the garment of salvation and robe of righteousness. God did not see their sin; He saw that an innocent sacrifice took their place. Something died that they could life. And so from the beginning, human beings haveknown to approach God through the blood covenant. *It has always been this way.*

Adam Teaches His Sons

As time passed, Adam and Eve became the proud parents of two sons, Cain and Abel. Cain was the oldest and took up farming as a livelihood. Abel was a shepherd. Now Adam had to learn things the hard way about the spiritual facts of life. Wanting to spare his children the same heartache, he was obedient to teach them about the blood covenant. So in Genesis 4:3-4, we find the two boys bringing an offering to God.

Abel Accepts the Covenant

Abel brought the best lambs from his flock. God approved of Abel's offering because this was the way He established for sinful man to approach Him. Therefore, Abel was acceptable to God, not by his own goodness, but based on the innocent blood sacrifice. It was the divinely ordained substitutionary sacrifice that made Abel acceptable to God. When God looked down at Abel's offering, He saw the blood of the innocent sacrifice. *The blood was the evidence that the penalty for sin had been paid.* God counted Abel as righteous (in right standing with Him) because of his offering.

Hebrews 11:4 puts it this way, "By faith Abel offered to God a more acceptable sacrifice than Cain, through which he received approval as righteous, God bearing witness by accepting his gifts; he died, but through his faith he is still speaking" (RSV).

Cain Rejects the Covenant

Contrary to his younger brother, Cain rejected God's way. He rejected the blood covenant. Instead of bringing an innocent sacrifice, he brought the fruit of his own labor. Cain probably brought his very best but it represented his own good works. *But even Cain's best goodness could not measure up to a perfect, absolute holy God.*

You see, Cain was trying to approach God with his own self-righteousness and man has been trying that ever since. But just as God rejected Adam and Eve's fig leaves, He also rejected Cain's offering of fruit. *There was no evidence that the penalty for sin had been paid.* There was no blood of an innocent substitute to cover Cain's sins. The fruit offering could not satisfy God's violated justice. So the very best Cain had to offer of his own merit was not good enough. *It was sinful man trying to approach a holy God on his own good works rather than through the blood of an innocent substitutionary sacrifice.*

God's rejection angered Cain. He became outraged against God. However, instead of striking Cain dead, God gave him a chance to repent. God probably said something like, "Cain, it's just like I told your parents. Our fellowship is restored by My grace and through your faith in accepting My way. It is My gift, not your works. So instead of boasting about how good a farmer you are, just accept My provision for you. If you don't, your own pride will destroy you." (see Genesis 4:5-7.)

Well, Cain wouldn't repent because evil had filled his heart. He would not confess his need for God's provision. When his pride turned to hate, he killed his brother. In First John 3:12 God confirms this condition of Cain's heart. He says, "Do not be like Cain, who belonged to the evil one (satan) and murdered his brother. And why did he murder him? Because his own actions were evil and his brother's were righteous" (NIV).

God was left with no choice but to drive Cain from His presence (see Gen. 4:8-16). Cain's descendants turned their back on the blood covenant and chose to follow their own evil ways (see Gen. 4:17-24). God gives a solemn reminder in Jude 11-13, that those who go the way of Cain will come to their end in everlasting gloom and darkness forever separated from God.

The Covenant Continued

God gave Adam and Eve another son to replace Abel. His name was *Seth*. Seth's descendants called upon the name of the Lord (see Gen. 4:26). They accepted God's covenant through blood and offered an innocent substitutionary sacrifice to cover their sins.

One of Seth's descendants was *Noah*. Noah walked with God and was the only righteous man in his generation (see Gen. 6:9). Therefore, when God destroyed the world because of its evil, He spared Noah and his family.

What do you think Noah did as his first act on dry land after the flood was over? He offered a sacrifice. God took notice and was pleased. It moved God to declare He would never again destroy every living creature even though man's heart is evil from his youth. (see Genesis 8:20-22.)

In Chapter 3 we saw that *Abraham* believed in the innocent blood sacrifice and was counted as righteous. *Isaac and Jacob* made sacrifices. (see Genesis 26:24-25; 31:54; 33:20; 35:7; 46:1.) This is why God could introduce Himself to Moses as the God of Abraham, Isaac and Jacob (see Exod. 3:15).

Moses asked the Pharaoh for permission to sacrifice (see Exod. 3:18). And then every believing Hebrew family offered a sacrifice to God as protection against the destroyer who took the life of the first born while the Hebrews were in Egypt.

So we see that from the very beginning of man's history, God ordained the innocent, substitutionary sacrifice as His means of helping man to understand His plan.

The Sacrifice System

Now He's going to make things even clearer by establishing an elaborate sacrifice system. The system would have five types of sacrifices. *Each sacrifice would uniquely reveal something about the nature of the final sacrifice when God would give Himself on man's behalf. Taken as a whole, they would form a complete picture of the perfect sacrifice. That way everybody would recognize Him when He came on the scene.*

This system called for 1,273 public sacrifices a year (see Num. 28-29). It included sacrifices each morning and evening, each Sabbath, the first day of each month and during the special feasts days of assembly and celebration. This amounts to almost 2,000,000 public sacrifice ceremonies from the time God established the system to the time He would come in the flesh as the perfect sacrifice. Then when He offered Himself, no more sacrifices would be needed.

In addition to the official public sacrifices, there were millions of individual offerings. Their number was staggering. So it was a continual blood bath. *God was making it clear that man can only approach Him through an innocent blood sacrifice.*

As a reminder, God does not require all this blood; sin requires it. Because God is holy and we are not; our sin separates us from Him. Because God loves us, He made a way for us to be reconciled to Him. With this background, let's now see how God maintained the blood covenant through the sacrifice system.

The Old Covenant

As just discussed, animal sacrifices date back to the most ancient times. They were a common form of worship from the earliest days of people's need for expressing their spiritual desires. The Law of God *(Torah)* incorporated this type of expression by providing for such offerings. Sacrifices were among the earliest and most profound expressions of the human desire to come as close as possible to God.

Unlike our modern understanding, for the Hebrews, a sacrifice to God meant something different than it means to the English speaker. For example, the word *sacrifice* in Webster's Dictionary gives the idea of giving up something of value as in giving a costly gift. We often speak of "making sacrifices."

However, the Hebrew word for sacrifice, *korban*, means to "come near." In this instance, it means the worshiper offers a sacrifice to God as an expression of his or her desire to draw near to God, not to appease God's wrath.

King David expressed this true meaning of sacrifice when he said, "But it is good for me to draw near to God..." (Ps. 73:28).

In the New Testament Scriptures, James expressed the same idea, "Draw near to God and He will draw near to you" (James 4:8).

When people brought a *Korban*, the offering showed them what they deserved if God were to judge them severely. However, God is a merciful God. He is not a vengeful, bloodthirsty deity who demands blood to appease His anger. This is a pagan concept of God.

God gave the sacrificial system as a means of restoring and purifying humankind's moral and spiritual nature. The sacrifice represents the death of humankind's carnal life and desires and through the ultimate sacrifice of Jesus, the restoration of fellowship with God.

The five types of offerings were: Sin Offering; Trespass Offering; Burnt Offering; Meal Offering; Peace Offering. These offerings were to be the physical outward expressions of the longings of the inward heart in seeking communion with God.

The Sin Offering and Trespass Offering were *mandatory offerings* associated with the sins of the nation and the individual Hebrew. The Burnt Offering, Meal Offering, and Peace Offering were spontaneous voluntary offerings of praise and thanksgiving. They were not associated with the individual's sins but were part of his or her worship to God. Therefore, God was pleased with these voluntary offerings and considered them a sweet aroma.

It's interesting that three out of five (60 percent) of these offerings were associated with praise and worship rather than sin. I believe this is what God expects to see today in the lives of individual believers and in the worship services of the congregational meetings. God wants joyous praise and worship.

The author of Hebrews 13:15 has these same offerings in mind when he wrote, "By Him (Jesus) let us offer the sacrifice of praise to God continually, that is, the fruit of our lips giving thanks to His name" (KJV). Church services that are cold and indifferent have gotten that way because they have eliminated spontaneous praise from their meetings. This is true for individual believers as well.

The chart entitled "Old Covenant Sacrifice System" which is at the end of this Chapter highlights the main aspects of each offering. You will need to refer to it as we discuss the offerings in detail. Drawing from what you learned about the Tabernacle, put yourself in the role of a Hebrew as he brings his sacrifice to the Brazen Altar.

Sin Offering (Leviticus 4:1-5,13; 6:24-30)

Let's begin with the Sin Offering. You present the Sin Offering to God because you are a sinner. The Ten Commandments make that very clear. Oh, you've tried hard enough to keep them, but you couldn't. There was something within you that caused you to fall short of their demands. Maybe you've never killed anybody, but you probably wanted to on occasion. And that is what the Commandments are all about. They were concerned with what you wanted to do and not so much with what you actually did.

> *You see, we are not a sinner because we sin; but we sin because we are a sinner. That's who we are in our core being. It's our nature. We inherited it from Adam. While people can do good things; we are not basically good. And in order to approach a holy God, we must have a Sin Offering.*

Making the Offering

The offering you bring must be spotless, with no defects or blemishes. You see, the animal foreshadows the perfect sacrifice that will come later. It is a picture of a person so it cannot be corrupted or imperfect in any way.

As you bring your offering to the Altar, the priest is waiting to meet you. You place your offering on the Altar and lay (heavily lean) your hands on the head of the animal and kill it. *In this way, you personally identify with the animal.* This is not just a meaningless ritual. You understand that your sins are symbolically being transmitted to this animal and that he is dying in your place. As you feel him dying on your behalf, you are grateful for the inno-cent substitutionary sacrifice. Except for the mercy of God, you would be on that Altar.

As you kill the animal, the priest standing with you catches the blood. He sprinkles some of it on the horns of the Altar and pours out what is left at the base of the Altar.

Because this is a Sin Offering, the sacrifice has to be taken out-side the camp away from the presence of God. The priest takes the carcass of the animal beyond the gate and outside the camp to a place where ashes are brought from the Altar. God has declared this place to be ceremonially clean because of the ashes. This is because the ashes indicate that an offering has been made and sin has been dealt with.

The priest was always rewarded for the service he performed. Except for his portion, the entire animal was burned outside the camp at the place of ashes. The entire animal had to be burned because it represented sin. God consumed the whole sacrifice.

You get none of the offering yourself because that would indi-cate communion with God, and God cannot commune where sin is represented.

Trespass Offering (Leviticus 5:14-19; 7:1-10)

Whereas the Sin Offering deals with your position before God, the Trespass Offering addresses your *walk with God*. You offer it for the sins you have committed, rather than for sin itself. Because you are a sinner, you sin. When you do, you need to bring a Trespass Offering.

As you lay your hands on the offering identifying your-self with it, you confess your particular sin. Your statement of confession offered to God is, "O Yahweh, I have sinned. I have done perversely. I have rebelled. I have committed (naming the sin). But I return in repentance and let this be for my atonement."

Confessing your sins removes the burden of guilt. It brings continuous forgiveness so that you can approach God with a clear conscience.

The priest offers the fat of the inward parts to God upon the Altar. He then sprinkles blood back and forth on the Altar and pours out the remainder at the base of the Altar.

The priest eats the remainder of the offering. You do not share in the offering because it is for sins you have committed.

Along with the offering, you must make *restitution* for any harm you may have done to a fellow Hebrew. This includes reimbursing him in full and adding twenty percent to the value of his loss. This brings about reconciliation between you and the one you have harmed.

The Cry of Your Heart

The Ten Commandments have helped you realize you are separated from God by your sins. This drives you to approach Him through the blood covenant. Through the Sin offering and Trespass Offering you express your *desire* for communion with God. You know that the blood of animals is only a temporary provision to cover your sins. But you are looking forward to the time when the perfect sacrifice will come to take them away once and for all.

Burnt Offering (Leviticus 1:3-17; 6:8-13)

Now that you have expressed a desire for communion with God, you want to offer yourself to Him. You indicate this through the Burnt Offering. The Burnt Offering expresses your *readiness for communion with God.* It is a voluntary offering of yourself. God doesn't force you to make this offering. You present yourself of your own free will. Yet, if you aren't willing to present yourself, it shows you aren't ready to have communion with God.

The offering you bring is a bull, lamb, or goat. If you are poor, you may bring a turtledove or pigeon. God's provision is for everyone. Furthermore, these are not wild animals, but domesticated pets you have personally raised. It really hurts you to kill them. It is truly agonizing. It is supposed to be a heart-felt emotional experience. As with all the offerings, they must be spotless, with no defects or blemishes.

As you bring the animal you have raised from its youth to the Altar, you lay your hands on its head to identify with it. If the offering is a lamb, you kill it on the *north side* of the Altar.

The priest catches the blood and sprinkles it round about and upon the Altar. Then the priest skins the animal to *expose all of its inward parts.* He then carefully dissects the animal checking each part to make sure it is free from defects. After the priest is satisfied with his examination, he burns the entire animal on the Altar, except for the skin.

The entire animal is offered as an expression of your readiness to present your entire being to God. It is a complete consecration or giving of yourself to God. Nothing can be held in reserve if you want to commune with Him. The smoke from the Burnt Offering ascends as a sweet aroma to God.

For his service, the priest receives the skin of the offering. The skin is the evidence that a sacrifice has been made. Since the entire sacrifice is offered to God, there is no portion left for you.

Meal Offering (Leviticus 2; 6:14-23)

At this point you've expressed a desire for communion with God through the Sin Offering and Trespass Offering. You then expressed a readiness for communion with God through the Burnt Offering. You now come to the Meal Offering.

If you use a King James Version of the Bible, you will notice the word "meat" is used instead of meal. This is because in King James' day, instead of inviting people to a meal, you would invite them to meat. This is the way they talked in those days. Today we invite people to a meal so we use our present-day terminology.

Now that you have expressed a desire and readiness to commune with God, you want to walk with Him and serve Him. The Meal Offering symbolizes your *walk in communion with God*.

The Meal Offering was the only offering without blood; however, it was only offered along with the Burnt Offering. The offering consisted of fine flour mingled with oil. Salt was added for seasoning and frankincense for spice. You offer it as raw flour, or as unleavened cakes and wafers that have been baked, fried, or roasted. No leaven or honey could be used in the flour.

Having properly prepared the offering, you present it to the priest. The priest offers a handful to God and eats the remainder. The handful represents the whole of the offering. By accepting the representative handful, God accepts the whole. The handful you offer to God is your way of saying you offer your whole life to God. Since the Meal Offering represents your walk with God by His might and power and for His glory alone, you do not share in the meal.

Peace Offering (Leviticus 3; 7:11-36)

By the time you come to the Peace Offering, you have expressed a desire for communion with God through the Sin Offering and Trespass Offering. You have expressed a readiness for communion through the Burnt Offering and Meal Offering. You are now going to *celebrate* that communion through the Peace Offering.

All the other offerings have been leading to the Peace Offering. This is the one you have been looking forward to presenting—because you are going to get a portion of this offering. It symbolizes the completion of your union with God. But first you had to be cleansed of your sins and offer your total being to God. Now that you have made that commitment, you are going to celebrate your union with God by sharing in the Peace Offering. This is what you've always wanted. This is why you made the other offerings. Through the Peace Offering, the cry and yearning of your heart is met as you enter into communion with God by sharing in the offering.

With a noticeable anticipation, you hurriedly lay your hands on the head of the animal and kill it. The priest catches the blood and sprinkles it all around and upon the Altar. He then takes the fat, places it on the Altar and offers it to God.

With the help of the priest, you now offer to God the *breast and right shoulder* of your sacrifice. The breast represents your heart; the right shoulder, your strength. The priest places his hands under yours, and together you move the sacrifice up and down, right and left, in a waving motion resembling a "T." God then gives back this portion. The High Priest receives the breast and the right shoulder goes to the priest who is helping you make the offering.

Along with the animal sacrifice, you also bring unleavened cakes and wafers mixed with oil plus loaves of leavened bread. There, in the courtyard of the Tabernacle, you eat the remainder of the sacrifice along with the loaves with your family and friends. It is a time of great joy as together you celebrate communion with God.

Because God has returned part of the offering to you, you now are symbolically feeding on His divine nature. He is coming into you and you into Him. You are becoming one with God. That's just what you have always wanted…to know God and share in His very own divine nature…to become one with Him. And now it's happening in the Peace Offering. It's the ultimate symbolism of your union with God.

The Old and the New

But it is only symbolism. It isn't the real thing. *It pointed you to the real thing, but it is not the real thing.* It is inadequate because you have to keep bringing the sacrifice again, and again and again. The blood of bulls and goats can only cover your sins, it cannot take them away. The blood of bulls and goats cannot make you righteous. It is not the "true meat" and "true drink" that satisfies the longing of your heart to have personal union and communion with God. It is not the promised seed (singular) of Abraham who would be a blessing to the whole world.

The New Covenant

But in the fullness of time, God sent forth His Son, born of a woman, born as a Jew (see Gal. 4:4). All the fullness of God dwelled in Him (see Col. 1:19; 2:9). God was in the Messiah reconciling the world unto Himself (see 2 Cor. 5:19). God had come to earth in the man Jesus to pay the penalty for sin on our behalf. He came to purchase our salvation with His own blood.

Jesus is the one for whom Adam and Eve were waiting. The skins of the innocent animals covering their bodies were a constant reminder that He would come. Jesus is that more acceptable sacrifice in whom Abel put his trust. Jesus is the substitute offering that renewed the covenant with Seth and his descendants. Jesus is Noah's sacrifice that moved God to put a rainbow in the sky. Jesus is the one Abraham believed in and was counted as righteous. Jesus is the reason God was the God of Abraham, Isaac, and Jacob. Jesus is Moses' sacrifice before Pharaoh. Jesus is the Passover Lamb that delivered the Hebrews from Egypt. Jesus is the New Covenant sacrifice who takes away the sins of the world. He is the one the Old Covenant sacrifices pointed to so that everyone would recognize Him when He arrived on the scene.

You see, God knew exactly what He was going to do when He would come to offer Himself. This is why He gave such specific details on how to offer each sacrifice. He would perfectly fulfill them in Jesus.

If you wanted someone to recognize you, you would tell them everything about you. Then when you arrived on the scene, they would know who you are.

This is how the entire Old Covenant (Testament) points to Jesus. This is how Jesus could say that everything written in the Law of Moses, in the Prophets, and the Psalms were about Him (Luke 24:44). This is how Jesus, on the road to Emmaus, could quote passage after passage beginning with the book of Genesis and going right through the Scriptures, explaining what the passages meant and what they said about Himself (see Luke 24:27).

The chart titled "The New Covenant Sacrifice" which is at the end of this chapter, shows how each Old Covenant offering pointed to Jesus. It also shows how each offering relates to a believer's relationship to Jesus. Refer to the chart for this discussion.

Sin Offering

We instinctively know that all have sinned and come short of the glory of God (see Rom. 3:23). The penalty for our sin is death (see Rom. 6:23). Therefore, we need a Sin Offering to reconcile us to God. Jesus is our Sin Offering. Because He had never sinned, He was a perfect sacrifice without spot or blemish (1 Peter 1:18-20).

In the Sin Offering, the blood on the horns of the Altar looked ahead to the blood of Jesus on the cross. As the blood was poured out at the foot of the Altar, all His blood was poured out at the foot of the cross. To fulfill the Sin Offering, Jesus went *beyond the gate* of the Temple, outside the camp which was the city of Jerusalem. (See Hebrews 13:11-12.) There, high upon a hill called Calvary; God sent fire into His bones. (see Lamentations 1:13.)

He gave Himself for our sins and bore our sins in His body. He was wounded for our transgressions and bruised for our iniquities. God laid (heavily leaned) on Him the iniquity of us all. (see Isaiah 53). The total sacrifice was consumed as He became sin for us (see 2 Cor. 5:21). God the Father could not look upon Him as our Sin Offering. Jesus, as our Sin Offering, cried out from the Cross, "...My God, my God, why hast thou forsaken me" (Matt. 27:46 KJV).

Jesus, as the Son of Man, our human representative, took on our sin nature when He became sin for us. He became who we are. In terms of a blood covenant, we exchanged natures at the cross. Remember from Chapter 2 that the robe represents the person. When Jesus was crucified, He took on our robe of self-righteousness, which is our sin nature. And our sin nature is like filthy rags to God (see Isa. 64:6).

God considers we who claim Jesus' death on our behalf, as being crucified with Him. Our sins are no longer put to our account. They were put to His account on the cross. Therefore, God does not see us as sinners. He sees us clean at the place of ashes, which is the cross of Jesus. The greatest horror story in the history of the world is when a person chooses to pay for his own sins by rejecting Jesus as his sacrifice.

We approach God through faith in the blood of Jesus, not by trying to keep the Ten Commandments. (see Galatians 2:16-21; 3:15-25.) When we accept Jesus as our Savior and Lord we give Him our heart (not mental credence), which represents our inward most parts. In exchange, He gives us His nature, which is without spot or blemish. It is pure and holy, therefore acceptable to God. His righteousness is imputed or counted to us. God sees us with the righteousness of Jesus (see 2 Cor. 5:21). Therefore, there is no condemnation to those who are in Jesus (see Rom. 8:1). They shall not come into condemnation but have passed from death to life (see John 5:24).

Looking ahead to this point in time, the prophet Isaiah wrote, "I will greatly rejoice in the Lord, my soul shall be joyful in my God; for he hath clothed me with the garment of salvation, he hath covered me with the robe of righteousness..." (Isa. 61:10 KJV).

> *This is what no animal could do. Animals could only "symbolically" represent us. But Jesus was our "real" representative. The writer of Hebrews explains:*

The old system of Jewish laws gave only a dim foretaste of the good things Christ [Messiah] would do for us. The sacrifices under the old system were repeated again and again, year after year, but even so they could never save those who lived under their rules. If they could have, one offering would have been enough; the worshipers would have been cleansed once for all, and their feelings of guilt would be done. But just the opposite happened: those yearly sacrifices reminded them of their disobedience and guilt instead of relieving their minds. For it is not possible for the blood of bulls and goats really to take away sins.

> *That is why Christ [Messiah] said, as he came into the world, 'O God, the blood of bulls and goats cannot satisfy you, so you have made ready this body of mine for me to lay as a sacrifice upon your altar. You were not satisfied with the animal sacrifices, slain and burnt before you as offerings for sin.'*
>
> *Then I said, "See, I have come to do your will, to lay down my life, just as the Scriptures said that I would." After Christ [Messiah] said this, about not being satisfied with the various sacrifices and offerings required under the old system, he then added, "Here I am. I have come to give my life." He cancels the first system in favor of a far better one.*
>
> *Under this new plan we have been forgiven and made clean by Christ's [Messiah's] dying for us once and for all. Under the old agreement the priests stood before the altar day after day offering sacrifices that could never take away our sins. But Christ [Messiah] gave himself to God for our sins as one sacrifice for all time, and then sat down in the place of highest honor at God's right hand, waiting for his enemies to be laid under his feet. For by that one offering he made*

forever perfect in the sight of God all those whom he is making holy.

And the Holy Spirit testifies that this is so, for he has said, this is the agreement I will make with the people of Israel, though they broke their first agreement: I will write my laws into their minds so that they will always know my will, and I will put my laws in their hearts so that they will want to obey them. And then he adds, I will never again remember their sins and lawless deeds. Now, when sins have once been forever forgiven and forgotten, there is no need to offer more sacrifices to get rid of them.

And so, dear brothers, now we may walk right into the very Holy of Holies where God is, because of the blood of Jesus. This is the fresh, new, life-giving way which Christ [Messiah] has opened for us by tearing the curtain—his human body—to let us into the holy presence of God (Hebrews 10:1-20 TLB).

For an Old Covenant teaching of a sacrifice being offered and coming back to life, see the story of the two birds in Leviticus 14. This points to the Messiah coming from heaven, being crucified and resurrected and returning to heaven bearing His own blood as the final sin offering.

Now that we have been crucified with our Lord, we no longer have to serve sin. It no longer may have dominion over us. We have been set free by the blood of Jesus (see Rom. 6). Paul expresses this freedom that all Christians may experience in Jesus. He says, "I have been crucified with Christ [Messiah]; it is no longer I who live, but Christ [Messiah] who lives in me; and the life I now live in the flesh I live by faith in the Son of God, who loved me and gave himself for me" (Gal. 2:20 RSV).

(Jesus as our Sin Offering: Galatians 1:4; 1 Corinthians 15:3; 2 Corinthians 5:21; Hebrews 9-10; 13:8-15; 1 Peter 2:24; Isa. 53.)

Trespass Offering

Jesus not only took on our sin nature, but He also took on all the sins that we have or will ever commit. He died not only for who we are but also for what we do. In the Sin Offering, Jesus destroyed the power of sin over us. We no longer need to serve our old nature because it was crucified with Jesus. Yet, we still sin. When we do, we need a Trespass Offering. Jesus is our Trespass Offering. Second Corinthians 5:19 says, "For God was in Christ [Messiah] restoring [reconciling] the world to himself, no longer counting men's sins against them but blotting them out. This is the wonderful message he has given us to tell others" (TLB).

Colossians 1:14 says we have forgiveness of sins through the blood of Jesus. *His perfect sacrifice included forgiveness for every sin you committed in the past, every sin you are now committing, and every sin you will commit in the future.* To help us realize this extent of God's forgiveness, Paul writes, "And you, being dead in your sins and the uncircumcision of your flesh, hath he [God] quickened together with him [Jesus] having forgiven you all trespasses; blotting out the handwriting of ordinances that was against us, which was contrary to us, and took it out of the way, nailing it to his cross" (Colossians 2:13-14 KJV).

God has forgiven us for all our sins because all of them; past, present, and future, were nailed to the cross of Jesus. Not only has God forgiven us for all our sins, but He doesn't even remember them. He blotted them from His memory. This is what the blood of bulls and goats could not do. We just read of this truth in Hebrews. It says, "because by one sacrifice he has made perfect forever those who are being made holy." Then he adds, "Their sins and lawless acts I will remember no more" (Hebrews 10:14,17 NIV).

When we sin, 'the Holy Spirit convicts us of that sin, but He doesn't condemn us. Neither should we condemn ourselves. We have total forgiveness through Jesus as our Trespass Offering. Therefore, to keep from condemning ourselves and carrying a burden of guilt, we confess our sins and claim the forgiveness that is already ours.

First John 1:6-9 sums this up for us. It says, "If we say we have fellowship with him while we walk in darkness, we lie and do not live according to the truth; but if we walk in the light, as he is in the light, we have fellowship with one another and the blood of Jesus his Son cleanses us from all sin. If we confess our sins, he is faithful and just, and will forgive our sins and cleanse us from all unrighteousness" (1 John 1: 6-9 RSV).

We stay free of condemnation and guilt by confessing our sins to God and claiming the forgiveness that is already ours through the blood of Jesus. Just like the Old Covenant believer, we say, "Heavenly Father, I have sinned. I have done perversely, and I have rebelled. I have committed *(naming the sin)*. But I return in repentance and claim my forgiveness through the blood of Jesus. He is my atonement."

Along with our confession to our heavenly Father, we must also confess our sins and make restitution to anyone we may have harmed by our sins. Jesus spoke of this in Matthew 5:23-24, "So, when you are offering your gift at the altar and remember that your brother holds something against you, leave your gift there at the altar and go and become reconciled to your brother; then come and offer your gift" (MLB).

Paul writes, "If you are angry, don't sin by nursing your grudge. Don't let the sun go down with you still angry—get over it quickly; for when you are angry you give a mighty foothold to the devil" (Eph. 4:26-27 TLB).

You see, when we get angry at someone and don't confess it, we begin to harbor that anger, that resentment, that envy, or jealousy. And it hardens our heart. When this happens, the root of bitterness takes hold. That's just the foothold satan needs to destroy us and create strife and enmity between us and another person.

Well, God has a better life for us than that. So He says in Ephesians 4:31-32, "Get rid of all bitterness among you—bad temper, anger, clamor, abusive language and all malice. Be kind toward one another, tenderhearted, forgiving one another, even as God has in Christ forgiven you" (MLB).

For spiritual as well as physical healing, James writes, "Therefore, confess your sins to one another, and pray for one another, that you may be healed" (James 5:16 RSV).

(Jesus as our Trespass Offering: 2 Corinthians 5:18-19; Colossians 1:14; 2:13-14; 1 John 1:6-9.)

Going on with God

Many people have expressed a desire to commune with God by accepting Jesus as their Sin Offering and Trespass Offering. They realized they could not save themselves and so they turned to Jesus as their Savior. Yet they are not experiencing the abundant covenant life the Bible promises. They are not enjoying the spiritual blessings God has for them. Their position with God may be secure but the glory of God is not manifested in their life. *This happens to believers because they have not appropriated Jesus as their Burnt Offering, Meal Offering, and Peace Offering.*

Often when this is brought to a believer's attention, they will say, "Well, I'm not ready to make that commitment." What they are really saying is, "I've expressed a desire for communion with God but I'm not ready to enter into it." Remember that these are voluntary offerings of praise and thanksgiving. They are not associated with our sin, but with our worship to God. God won't force us to worship Him. We must choose to do so of our own free will. Yet the only way to experience the abundant life Jesus promised is by expressing our readiness to have it through these, the commitment pictured in these offerings....

Burnt Offering

Jesus voluntarily left His home in glory to become our Burnt Offering (see Phil. 2:5-8). *As the animal was killed on the north side of the Altar, Jesus, too, was crucified on the north side of Jerusalem.* He perfectly fulfilled in His body every detail of the Old Covenant. In the Burnt Offering, the entire animal was offered to God. Likewise, Jesus said, "For 1 came down from heaven, not to do my own will, but the will of him that sent me" (John 6:38 KJV). On another occasion He said, "...My nourishment is that I do the will of Him who sent Me and completely do His work" (John 4:34 MLB). Paul was recognizing Jesus as our Burnt Offering when he wrote, "... Christ [Messiah] loved us and gave himself up for us, a fragrant offering and sacrifice to God" (Eph. 5:2 RSV).

As Jesus offered Himself to God with no reservations, so must we do the same. Paul puts it this way, "I appeal to you therefore, brethren, by the mercies of God to present your bodies as a living sacrifice, holy and acceptable to God, which is your spiritual worship. Do not be conformed to this world but be transformed by the renewal of your mind, that you may prove what is the will of God, what is good and acceptable and perfect" (Rom. 12:1-2 RSV).

We present ourselves as a living sacrifice by yielding to the Lordship of Jesus over our lives. It takes many believers a lifetime and some never realize that Jesus is not just our friend who came to help us out when we are in trouble. Jesus came to take over our lives. Our relationship to Him is one of Lord and servant.

As our Lord, He is the master, ruler and controller of our life. We are His purchased possession. He bought and paid for us with His own blood (see Eph. 1:14). Therefore, Paul writes, "Do you not know that your body is a temple of the Holy Spirit within you, which you have from God? You are not your own; you were bought with a price. So glorify God in your body" (1 Cor. 6:19-20 RSV).

As a Burnt Offering, we lay ourselves open for God to inspect us. Our prayer must be, "Search me, O God, and know my heart: try me, and know my thoughts: and see if there be any wicked way in me, and lead me in the way everlasting" (Ps. 139:23-24 KJV).

(Jesus as our Burnt Offering: Psalm 40:6-8; John 4:34; Ephesians 5:2; Hebrews 9-10.)

Meal Offering

On one occasion Jesus said, "...Except a grain of wheat fall into the ground and die, it abideth alone: but if it die, it bringeth forth much fruit" (John 12:24 KJV). Jesus was speaking of His death and resurrection. Through it He perfectly fulfilled the Meal Offering by becoming the bread of life for us to feed on.

The Meal Offering symbolizes our walk in communion with God. Speaking of His walk with the Father, Jesus said, "...I always do those things that please him" (John 8:29 KJV). In the Bible, leaven represents sin. Honey, when used with leaven, represents the pleasures of sin. (see Matthew 16:6; 1 Corinthians 5:6-8; Revelation 10:9-10.) As the perfect Meal Offering, Jesus knew no sin (see 2 Cor. 5:21). There was no leaven or honey in His life. It was as the sweet fragrance of incense to His heavenly Father.

The Bible uses oil as a symbol of the Holy Spirit. In place of the leaven and honey, Jesus was full of the Holy Spirit. As oil was poured on the flour of the Meal Offering, it was also poured upon Jesus. When He was water baptized, the heavens were opened to Him and He saw the Spirit of God descending like a dove and lighting upon Him. God then spoke and said, "... This is my beloved Son, in whom I am well pleased" (Matt. 3:17).

When He began His ministry, Jesus said, "The Spirit of the Lord is upon me, because he hath anointed me to preach the gospel to the poor; he hath sent me to heal the brokenhearted, to preach deliverance to the captives, and recovery of sight to the blind, to set at liberty them that are bruised, to preach the acceptable year of the Lord" (Luke 4:18-19 KJV).

Peter preached, "How God anointed Jesus of Nazareth with the Holy Spirit and with power; how he went about doing good and healing all that were oppressed by the devil, for God was with him" (Acts 10:38 KJV).

Salt preserves and purifies from corruption. *Believers are preserved, purified, and kept by the blood of Jesus.* He is able to keep us from falling and present us faultless before the presence of God's glory with exceeding joy. (see Jude 24.) This is the "sealing" with the Holy Spirit when we ask Jesus into our life. (See Ephesians 1:13; 4:30; 2 Corinthians 1:22; 1 Peter 1:5.) In this regard, salt relates to our position with God.

But it also relates to our walk with God. In Matthew 5:13, Jesus said, "You are the salt of the earth." But He went on to say, "But if the salt has lost its taste, how shall its saltiness be restored? It is no longer good for anything except to be thrown out and trodden underfoot by men" (RSV).

Believers function as the salt of the earth when we appropriate Jesus as our Meal Offering. As there was no leaven or honey found in Him, neither should there be any found in us. This means to walk with God in the power of the Holy Spirit.

You see, God, through the Holy Spirit, will not lead us into temptation (James 1:13). Therefore, when we walk in the Spirit, we shall not fulfill the lust of the flesh. We will not be tempted to sin. This means there will be no sin in us. Since we live in the Spirit we should also walk in the Spirit. (See Galatians 5:16-25.) To make the Meal Offering a reality in our life, Paul writes for all Christians, "...to be filled with the Spirit" (Eph. 5:18 KJV). The Holy Spirit is God come to live in us. *Only when we allow Him to control our life, can we experience fellowship with God.*

When we experience fellowship with God, we find it to be sweeter than any honey the world can offer. It creates a desire within us to set our affections on things that are above rather than earthly gains and earthly things (see Col.3:1-3). It becomes our motivation to want to come out from among the world and be separate (see 2 Cor. 6:17). It moves us to be holy as He is holy (see 1 Pet. 1:16) that we may glorify and bring honor to Him who has brought us out of darkness into His marvelous light (see 1 Pet. 2:9). Then as frankincense, our lives will be a sweet fragrance to our heavenly Father.

(Jesus as our Meal Offering: John 4:34; 8:29; 12:23-24; Luke 4:18; Ephesians 5:2; 1 Peter 2:22).

Peace Offering

When Jesus was born, all of heaven gave praise to God saying, "Glory to God in the highest, and on earth peace to men on whom his favor rests" (Luke 2:14 NIV). *God's favor rests on all who have accepted Jesus as their Peace Offering.*

He is the "true meat" and "true drink" that satisfies the cries and longings of the human heart. (see John 6:53-63.) This is the offering we have been looking for. All the other offerings were leading up to this one. We get a portion of this offering. And the portion we get is God's very own divine nature coming in us by the person of the Holy Spirit (see 2 Pet. 1:4).

In the Peace Offering, the breast and right shoulder that were waved before God in a "T" motion, looked ahead to the cross of Jesus. There His heart melted like wax. His strength drained away like water and dried up like sun-baked clay. (See Psalm 22:14-15.) But as the breast and shoulder were given back to the priest, so also were they given back to Jesus. Now He ministers in the heavenly Holy of Holies as our High Priest. There, before our Heavenly Father, Jesus bears our name over His heart and on His shoulder. *Through His intercession on our behalf, we can cast all our cares upon Him, for He cares for us* (see 1 Pet. 5:7). We can endure all things through our Lord who strengthens us (see Phil. 4:13).

As the Peace Offering was eaten with leavened bread and unleavened bread mixed with oil, so we who know sin have received within us He who did not know sin. The Holy Spirit is the heavenly oil of joy and gladness who has come to live in our heart.

At one time we were separated from God by our sins. Being apart from God, we were restless with no peace in our hearts. But now through the blood of Jesus we may draw near to God. We may walk in communion and fellowship with Him. *We may walk in peace with Him and with each other. His peace may rule our troubled hearts.*

Jesus said,

> *Peace I leave with you; my peace I give unto you: not as the world giveth, give I unto you. Let not your heart be troubled, neither let it be afraid. These things I have spoken unto you, that in me ye might have peace. In the world ye shall have tribulation: but be of good cheer I have overcome the world* (John 14:27; 16:33 KJV).

(Jesus as our Peace Offering: Luke 2:14; John 14:27; 16:33; Romans 5:1; Ephesians 2:11-19; Colossians 1:16-23; 3:15).

Worship Is a Person

When Jesus gave Himself as the perfect sacrifice, He fulfilled the Old Covenant pictures that pointed to Himself. This does not mean He did away with it. It means He was and is the true spiritual reality of the pictures. We don't worship a system (religion) but a person. Jesus of Nazareth (Messiah Yeshua) is that person. He is the sacrifice needed for cleansing. Speaking of Himself through King David, God said, "Sacrifice and offering Thou dost not desire; mine ears hast Thou opened: burnt-offering and sin-offering hast Thou not required. Then said I, Lo, I come: in the volume of the book it is written of me." (see Psalm 40:6-7; Hebrews 10:5-8.)

Both Jew and Gentile may enter into the New Covenant through the blood of Jesus, the once and for all perfect sacrifice.

OLD COVENANT SACRIFICE SYSTEM						
OFFERING	**NATURE**	**OFFERER'S WORK**	**PRIEST'S WORK**	**GOD'S WORK**	**PRIEST'S PORTION**	**OFFERER'S PORTION**
SIN	Bull-lamb-goat turtledove pigeon	Lay on hands Kill animal	Sprinkle blood on altar	The whole within— without camp	A portion not burned	None
TRESPASS	Ram	Lay on hands Kill animal	Sprinkle blood on altar	Fat of inwards	Remainder	None
BURNT	Bull-lamb-goat turtledove pigeon	Lay on hands Kill animal	Sprinkle blood on altar	Burn all on altar	Skin	None
MEAL	Fine flour Oil-salt No leaven Honey	Bring to priest	Offer handful	Handful	Remainder	None
PEACE	Bull-lamb-goat	Lay on hands Kill animal	Sprinkle blood on altar	Fat of inwards	Breast and shoulder	Remainder

THE NEW COVENANT SACRIFCE		
OFFERING	**JESUS CHRIST**	**THE BELIEVER**
SIN	Forgiveness for sinner we are by becoming sin for us	Crucified with Christ
TRESPASS	Forgiveness for sins we commit by taking sins on Himself	Confess our sins for reconciliation
BURNT	Completely gave Himself to the Father	Present ourselves to Jesus as Lord
MEAL	Walked in obedience to the Father	Walk in the Spirit
PEACE	Had perfect fellowship with Father	Communion and fellowship with God

Chapter 6

THE HIGH PRIEST

Background

In our previous two chapters, we learned that when God gave the law, He also established a Tabernacle, a sacrifice system, and a priesthood. The Tabernacle was a physical representation showing the people how to approach God. Tabernacle worship centered on the offerings. Each offering uniquely revealed something about the nature of the final sacrifice when God would give Himself on man's behalf.

God chose Aaron and his sons to serve Him as priests (see Exod. 28:1; 29:9). The priesthood was to be exclusively theirs. No one else could function in the priestly office. Aaron was the first High Priest. At his death, he would be succeeded by his oldest son. This way the priesthood could be passed down from generation to generation. Aaron's sons were to begin their priestly responsibilities at the age of 30 (see Num. 4:3).

When Aaron and his sons were consecrated, or set apart for their priestly office, they along with their priestly garments were sprinkled with blood. (see Exodus 28-29; Leviticus 8). This was a necessary part of the ceremony because they were sinners. You see, the priests were to be the mediators between God and man. Yet God, in His holiness, could not receive them unless their sins were covered by blood. Their blood-sprinkled garments publicly testified to their real inadequacy to represent the people. Yet it pointed the entire nation to a future time, when a perfect priest would come. He would set Himself apart and give His own blood as the perfect mediator between God and man. We'll learn about that perfect priest in this chapter.

The Old Covenant

High Priestly Garments (Exodus 28)

The central figure in the Old Covenant system was the *High Priest*. He was the most important person in the entire nation because he represented the nation before God.

The High Priest stood out above everyone else. This was not only because of his office, but also because of his *dress*. He wore seven different pieces of clothing. In the Bible, the number seven represents perfection. So symbolically, the High Priest was perfectly clothed for his position.

His garments consisted of fine linen beautifully interwoven with blue, gold, scarlet, and purple. They were called "holy" garments (see Exod. 28:2). Their glory and beauty gave the proper dignity and honor to the High Priestly office. *They also uniquely revealed something about the nature of the perfect High Priest who was to come.* Like the sacrifices, when taken as a whole, they formed a complete picture of the one who would be greater than Aaron.

The High Priest wore *white breeches of fine linen* next to his body. Over the linen breeches, he wore a *white coat of fine linen* that hung to his feet. This was his ordinary dress as well as the dress of the other priests. Therefore, they were not considered part of his garments of glory and beauty. In the Bible, fine white linen represents perfect righteousness. So from within, the High Priest was symbolically clothed in perfect righteousness.

The High Priest wore a *blue robe over his coat.* The blue color speaks of heaven. It represents a heavenly appointment by God Himself who selected Aaron as the High Priest. The blue robe hung to slightly above the white coat. Embroidered on the bottom of the robe were *golden bells* alternating with pomegranates of blue, purple, and scarlet. Gold represents deity. The purple and scarlet refer to royalty and blood sacrifice. These colors pointed ahead to the time when God Himself would come from heaven to establish a kingdom with His own blood.

As the High Priest walked back and forth inside the Tabernacle, the people outside could not see him. But they could hear the bells jingling. And as long as they heard the bells jingling, they knew the High Priest was alive and representing them before God.

Over his robe, the High Priest wore a short sleeveless jacket, called an *ephod*. The ephod was made of beaten gold that had been cut into thin wires and woven into fine linen of blue, purple, and scarlet. It consisted of two pieces, front and back, that were joined at the shoulders by two gold chains. Two onyx stones were set in gold and fastened to the ephod at the shoulders. The names of the 12 tribes of Israel were engraved with a seal on these stones, six names on each stone.

The ephod reached from the shoulders to below the waist, hanging to slightly above the blue robe. A *sash* of fine linen fastened around the ephod. The sash served as a reminder that the High Priest was a servant of both God and the nation of Israel.

A gold *breastplate*, also of blue, purple and scarlet was attached to the ephod. Twelve beautiful stones were attached to the breastplate. The name of one of the 12 tribes was engraved with a seal on each stone. The stones were attached in four rows with three stones to a row.

As the High Priest interceded for the people, he symbolically carried the entire covenant nation into the presence of God. The stones on his shoulders symbolized his strength. Those over his heart represented his love.

The seventh article of clothing was a *turban (mitre)* worn as a headpiece. A gold plate was attached to the turban with a blue ribbon. The words "HOLINESS TO THE LORD" were engraved with a seal on the gold plate. It was the crowning piece of the garments of glory and beauty. By wearing it on his forehead, the High Priest would symbolically bear the guilt of any unclean sacrifices made to God. It also made him acceptable before God.

So we see that when the High Priest was set apart for his office, he, along with his garments of glory and beauty, were sprinkled with blood. Then later as he ministered on behalf of the people, he stood before God as the holy and righteous representative of the entire covenant nation. *God accepted the people in their priest.*

The Day of Atonement

The High Priest had many duties and responsibilities, but his most important duty was to minister on the *Day of Atonement.* The Day of Atonement occurred on the tenth of Tishri, which is the seventh month on the Hebrew religious calendar. This corresponds to the Gentile months of September-October. The Day of Atonement is also known as the Day of Forgiveness. The Jews call it Yom Kippur.

The Day of Atonement is the most solemn of all days. This is the day for making atonement or covering for the sins of the entire nation of Israel. *It was the one day of the year when the High Priest could go behind the veil into the Holy of Holies.* There he would offer the blood of the sin offering on the Mercy Seat. God would accept it as covering for the sins of the people.

The pressure was on the High Priest. If he made a mistake, the whole nation would be without forgiveness. So God gave detailed instructions to the High Priest. The instructions not only told the High Priest what to do, *but they pointed the nation to a priest who would come as one greater than Aaron.* When he came, everyone would recognize Him *because He would perfectly fulfill every detail of these instructions in Himself.*

Leviticus 16 describes the ceremony on the Day of Atonement. I suggest you read it before continuing with this chapter. The High Priest is in complete charge of the service. He must perform all by himself. No one can help him or even touch him until the ceremony is completed.

As we follow the events step by step, put yourself in the role of a Hebrew. Come with me to the Tabernacle and together we will watch as our High Priest ministers on our behalf on the Day of Atonement.

High Priest Washes Himself Clean

The first action by the High Priest is to wash himself. The washing represents a *symbolic cleansing* of any ceremonial defilement. Therefore the High Priest is cleansed so that he might minister on behalf of the people. What a teaching that is for us. We must be spiritually and morally clean before we can minister God to others.

Dresses for the Service

After washing, the High Priest dresses for the service. He puts on his linen breeches, his white robe, his sash, and his turban. These are the clothes he will wear to represent the nation before God in the Holy of Holies. But notice that these *are not* his garments of glory and beauty. He does not put on his blue robe with the beautiful colors, golden bells, and pomegranates embroidered on the bottom. Neither does he put on his glorious ephod and breastplate.

On the contrary, he is dressed very plainly in his white coat of fine linen. *And he looks just like everybody else.* Why, you can't tell him from the next guy. As you look at him, you probably think to yourself, "What makes him so great anyway? After all, the only reason he is the High Priest is because he is a son of Aaron. He probably didn't even want to be a High Priest. But there he is following in his father's footsteps."

Makes Sin Offering for Himself

Now that he is properly dressed for the occasion, the High Priest begins the ceremony. His first action is to sacrifice a bull as his own sin offering. You see, the High Priest is just a man. So he must make atonement for his own sins before he can represent the nation. That doesn't give you too much confidence knowing that the person representing you before God is a sinner just like you are. Why, he's no better or worse than the rest of us.

But since he is a man, he does understand your problems. He can identify with you and you with him. You know he is sweating it out on your behalf. But it seems as soon as you get to know him, he dies. Then somebody else takes his place. And the new High Priest may not even like you. Well, this constant change with a mere human priest is very unsettling, but it's the best you've got.

Enters Holy Of Holies

After the High Priest makes his sacrifice, he takes some of the blood of the sacrifice and carries it inside the Tabernacle. He has now disappeared from your view. First he must pass through the outer room called the Holy Place. He goes by the Golden Candlestick and Shewbread Table but stops at the Incense Altar. There he puts coals from the Altar into a golden censer and fills his hand with incense. Then he goes behind the veil into the inner-room called the Holy of Holies.

We learned about the Holy of Holies in Chapter 4. Remember that the only piece of furniture in the Holy of Holies is the Ark of the Covenant. It is a small chest about two feet high, two feet wide, and four feet long. The lid attached to the Ark is called "The Mercy Seat." A replica of cherubim (angels) is attached to each end of the Mercy Seat. Their wings outstretch touching each other at the middle of the lid.

Right between the two cherubim and above the Mercy Seat is the blinding light representing the presence of God's glory.

It is the manifested presence of God dwelling in the midst of the people. The Holy of Holies is God's earthly throne room, the Mercy Seat is His throne, and the great light is His visible presence.

The glory of God is so bright in the Holy of Holies that the High Priest cannot stand in His presence. So as he goes into the room he puts incense over the hot coals in the golden censor. When the incense touches the coals, it completely fills the room with a fragrant white cloud of smoke. This enables the High Priest to enter into God's presence.

The fragrance of the incense is a sweet aroma to God. Standing in its midst, the High Priest sprinkles the blood of his sin offering over the Mercy Seat. This is the place of atonement for the sins of the nation. But before he can represent the nation, he must first make atonement for his own sins. Seven times he sprinkles the blood over the Mercy Seat. The number seven looks ahead to the perfect sacrifice that will come and not only cover sins, but take them away.

But until that time, the High Priest must enter the Holy of Holies on the Day of Atonement. And he must stand during the entire ceremony. There is no place for him to sit down because *his work is never finished.* I'm sure when he entered the Holy of Holies, he would look at the Mercy Seat and want to just sit down and put an end to this once and for all. Instead he has to keep going back year after year because his job is never finished.

To this point, the work of the High Priest has been for himself. But it is all leading up to the main event of the day, which is the sin offering for the nation. Now that he has made atonement for his own sins, he comes out of the Tabernacle back to the Altar in the outer courtyard.

Sin Offering for the Nation

Two goats are provided as one sin offering for the nation. One goat will be sacrificed to God while the other goat will be led into the wilderness. As the excitement builds, the High Priest brings the two goats before the Altar at the entrance of the Tabernacle. There he casts lots to determine which goat will die and which will be let go. After the lot is cast, he places one of the goats on the Altar, heavily leans his hands on its head and kills it. *The sins of the nation are symbolically being transmitted to this animal. He is dying in your place as he symbolically becomes your sin substitute.*

Then the High Priest takes the blood of the animal into the Holy of Holies. *This is the most crucial moment of the biggest event of the year.* Not only is the High Priest nervous, but you are nervous. You are particularly nervous when the High Priest disappears from your view back into the Tabernacle. You are worried; you are anxious; you are tense. You'd like to go in there with him and make sure he does it just right. You see, this is your sin he is atoning for. Why, he might have a heart attack when he comes into God's presence and nobody would know it. That inner veil separates the throne room of God from the rest of the people. You don't know what is going on because you can't see in.

Oh, he has tried to describe it to you but it's just too wonderful for words. It's too glorious. There's no way he can express how it feels to stand before the glory of God in the midst of the sweet cloud of incense.

If you could just go in yourself—but you can't. You can't even go into the outer room. Only the priest can go in there. You are stuck out in the courtyard. If this could just be completed once and for all, then you wouldn't have to keep bringing sacrifices over and over and over. You wouldn't have to sweat out the High

Priest year after year hoping God will accept him on your behalf. *Surely there must be a real Tabernacle, a real sacrifice, a real High Priest to put an end to this once and for all.*

But for now you must stand on the outside believing by faith that the blood of a goat is going to cover your sins and bring you forgiveness before God. Knowing that the High Priest has entered the Holy of Holies on your behalf, your heart begins to pound faster and faster.

Standing before God in the cloud of incense, the High Priest sprinkles the blood of the goat over the Mercy Seat. Under that Mercy Seat in the Ark of the Covenant are the stone tablets containing the Ten Commandments. These are the Commandments that you have broken. And every day of the year, God looks down from His glory cloud above the Ark and sees His laws that you have broken.

The broken law is evidence of your rebellion and sin. And the penalty for sin is death. God's holy justice must be satisfied. The price must be paid. But God in His great grace and mercy has made a provision so that you don't have to pay it. He has declared that the blood of the innocent sacrifice will take your place and cover your sins.

And now seven times the High Priest sprinkles the blood of the innocent substitutionary sacrifice over the Mercy Seat. At that moment, as God looks down from His cloud of glory, He doesn't see the evidence of your sins. Instead He sees the blood. The blood of the innocent sacrifice tells God that life has been given to pay the penalty. *The blood-covered Mercy Seat changes God's throne from one of judgment to one of mercy.* Justice has been administered. God's holy nature has been satisfied that the penalty for sin has been paid.

The High Priest then returns from inside the Tabernacle back into the courtyard. He goes directly to the Altar and smears the blood of the bull and goat on the horns of the Altar. Then he sprinkles the blood upon the Altar seven times. This is a ceremonial cleansing of the Altar from the sinfulness of the nation.

The Scapegoat

Now the High Priest needs some way to visibly show you that your sins have been dealt with and separated from you. This is the purpose of the second goat. The High Priest lays his hands on the goat symbolically transmitting to it, your sins and the sins of the nation. Then he sends the goat into the wilderness. And your sins symbolically go with it.

The scapegoat provides the picture of your sins being carried away. But the first goat had to be sacrificed and its blood sprinkled in the Holy of Holies. The blood of the first goat was the evidence to God that the penalty for your sin had been paid. *The second goat could carry away your sins only after the blood of the first goat had been applied. The second goat is actually pushed off a cliff, and symbolically, your sins are going with it away from God.*

Now the blood of the first goat represented you. Symbolically your blood was applied through that first goat. But you were standing on the outside and didn't see it happen. But now as you see the second goat taken into the wilderness, you know that you are forgiven and your sins have been separated from you. And that's the best news that you have heard since this time last year.

The High Priestly Garments

But just as you are becoming overjoyed with this glorious news the High Priest disappears again. He goes back into the Tabernacle to remove his plain white coat and to wash himself. Again, you begin to worry. Would God accept what the High Priest has done on your behalf? Are you really forgiven for another year? Is God pleased? How will you know? There is only one way. That's by hearing the jingling of the bells as the High Priest puts back on his garments of glory and beauty.

There in the Holy Place, hidden from your eyes, he puts on his beautiful blue robe with the gold bells and pomegranates. He puts on the ephod and breastplate with the stones bearing the name of your tribe. Symbolically he is carrying you on his shoulders and over his heart. As he walks around inside the Tabernacle, you hear the jingling of the bells. A peace comes over you as this is your evidence that your High Priest is still alive and soon coming out to meet you.

A Burnt Offering

Finally as the High Priest appears in his garments of glory and beauty, great shouts of joy go out from the people. You've been forgiven for another year. To conclude the ceremony, the High Priest offers a burnt offering to the Lord. It is a sacrifice of praise that God receives as a sweet aroma. All is well. *That is until next year, when it has to be done all over again.*

A Shadow of Better Things to Come

Once again we see the inadequacy of the Old Covenant system. It is true the Ten Commandments were perfect. But they were written on tablets of stone rather than the fleshly tablets of the people's heart. And the Tabernacle was just a temporary building. Although God gave the details for its construction, still it was made with the hands of man. God established the sacrifice system, yet the blood of bulls and goats could never really take away sins.

Therefore, the job of the High Priest was never finished. He had to keep going back year after year offering the sacrifices for his own sins and the sins of the people. Aaron and his sons were imperfect. But God in His grace, accepted the people in their High Priest as their holy and righteous representative.

The New Covenant

High Priestly Garments

But now a perfect High Priest has come to fulfill what the Old Covenant High Priest could not do. Philippians 2:5-11 tells us about this. It says that Jesus was in the form of God. This means that He had the same nature and attributes of God. In other words, He was God coming to us in human flesh. Other scriptures describe His preexisting glory. The prophet Isaiah saw Him high and lifted up on His throne, and His glory filled the heavenly Temple. Isaiah cried, "Woe is me, for mine eyes have seen the King, the Lord of hosts." (see Isaiah 6:1-5.)

Peter, James, and John saw Him on a high mountain. His appearance changed before their very eyes. His face did shine as the sun, His raiment was as white as the light. (see Matthew 17:2.)

John saw Him again in the book of Revelation. His head and hair were white like wool, as white as snow. His eyes were like a flame of fire. His feet were like fine brass. His voice was as the sound of many waters. His glory was an unapproachable light. To look upon Him was to look upon glittering diamonds and shining rubies. (see Revelation 1:14; 4:3; 1 Timothy 6:16.)

Yet our Lord did not cling to His pre-existing glory. Instead He laid aside His garments of glory and beauty. Now we've learned that in blood covenant the garment represents the person. God did not have a garment. *He laid aside His own glory to be a High Priest for us who would feel our infirmities and be tempted as*

171

we are (see Heb. 4:15). He would be a God we could identify with and who could identify with us. He is the One the High Priestly garments were pointing to.

Dresses for the Service

At the same time God laid aside His glory, He dressed Himself for the perfect atonement service. He dressed for the service by *preparing Himself a body* and becoming one of us. The Creator became the creation. The Master became the servant. The Son of God became the Son of Man. The Lord of Glory became a baby in a manger. And they called His name Jesus (Yeshua).

And He looked just like everybody else. Why, you couldn't tell Him from the next guy. He didn't have a halo around His head, you know. He wasn't glorious and beautiful in His appearance. He just wore a plain white linen robe. But no man spoke like this man, who was perfectly fulfilling the Old Covenant as He began His ministry at the age of 30 (see Luke 3:23).

Symbolic Washing

His first action was to allow John the Baptist to baptize Him in the Jordan River. In this way Jesus identified Himself with the Old Covenant High Priest who was washed in water on the day he was set apart for his priestly ministry.

But so we would understand that He really didn't need cleansing, Jesus said, "...I sanctify (cleanse) myself, that they also might be sanctified through the truth" (John 17:19 KJV). Earlier He had declared Himself to be the truth (see John 14:6).

The Sin Offering for the World

The High Priest after the seed of Aaron was a sinner just like everybody else. However, Jesus was a High Priest after the seed of

God. He was begotten of God the Father. He was very God but also very man.

He was perfectly righteous from within and knew no sin. Therefore, it was not necessary that He sacrifice for Himself. Instead He sacrificed Himself for us. He who knew no sin became sin for us (see 2 Cor. 5:21). He became that once and for all perfect sacrifice. He got up on the altar by His own free will. That altar was the cross. There He became the sin offering for the world. He humbled Himself and became obedient unto death, even the death of the cross.

On the morning of His resurrection, He appeared to Mary and said, "...Touch me not; for I am not yet ascended to my Father: but go to my brethren, and say unto them, I ascend unto my Father, and your father; and to my God and your God" (John 20:17 KJV). Like the Old Covenant High Priest no one could touch Jesus until He had completed His work.

But later that same evening Jesus appeared to His disciples and said, "See my hands and my feet, that it is I myself: handle me and see; for a spirit has not flesh and bones as you see that I have" (Luke 24:39 RSV).

Jesus said flesh and bone rather than flesh and blood. That's because all of His blood was poured out at the foot of the cross. But now that His work was over, they could touch Him. It happened just like it did in the Old Covenant except this was not the blood of a goat.

On resurrection morning, Jesusentered into that more perfect Tabernacle in heaven. He went right into the heavenly Holy of Holies. *It was the real High Priest, entering the real throne room of God, with the real sacrifice. The real sacrifice was His own blood that He sprinkled over the Mercy Seat.* With His blood, He purchased our eternal salvation. This is part of the will He has left us in the New Covenant in His blood.

Certificate of Debt

But when someone dies and leaves a will, there must be evidence of the death before the will can be executed. *The evidence that this will and the New Covenant can be executed is the blood of Jesus sprinkled on the Mercy Seat.* All who claim His death as their personal sin substitute receive the gift of the will, which is eternal life in union and communion with God.

When criminals were put in jail in Rome, their crimes and the number of years' penalty were listed and nailed to their cell door. Each year the jailer would go by the cell door and mark off the time served until the debt had been paid. This paper was called a Certificate of Debt. It stayed nailed to the cell door until the debt was paid in full. Then the jailer would take the Certificate of Debt to the judge who would stamp it "paid in full." Then the prisoner would be set free.

This is what God has done for all who will receive it. He took our Certificate of Debt that lists all our sins and He nailed it to the cross of Jesus. And when it was over, the Judge hanging on the cross cried out, "It is finished" (John 19:30). *This was His victory cry.* He meant that our sin debt had now been paid in full. When we appropriate this payment in our own life, we can be set free from the penalty and bondage of sin.

The Perfect Atonement

We have been forgiven and made clean once and for all by the blood of Jesus. He is the perfect sin offering. Through His blood, He has *forever* made us holy and righteous in the eyes of God. The blood of Jesus did what the blood of bulls and goats could never do. It didn't just cover sins; it took them away to be remembered no more. So He doesn't offer Himself again and again as the High Priest of the Old Covenant had to keep bringing the sin offering year after year.

If that was necessary, He would have to die again and again. But He came once, for all, to put away the power of sin forever. Just as it is destined that men die only once, and after that comes the judgment, so Jesus died only once as the offering for the sins of the world.

So when sins have been forgiven and forgotten, there is no need to offer more sacrifices to get rid of them. We are like the scapegoat. We are set free. *The blood of Jesus has removed our transgressions from us as far as the east is from the west* (see Ps. 103:12). Now the distance between east and west cannot be measured. It is infinite. So is the distance that the blood of Jesus has removed us from our sins. (see Hebrews 9-10.)

The angels must have shouted for joy that day when Jesus went into the heavenly Holy of Holies with His own blood. His wounded, pierced, bruised body was the final burnt offering. God the Father received the sacrifice of His only begotten Son as a sweet aroma. (see Ephesians 5:2.)

The High Priestly Garments

The veil of the glory of God has now been lifted off of Jesus. As our High Priest, He has now put back on His garments of glory and beauty. Hebrews 2:9 says, "But we see Jesus, who for a little while was made lower than the angels, crowned with glory and honor because of the suffering of death…" (RSV).

God the Father has exalted Him and given Him the name that is above every name. At the name of Jesus, every knee shall bow and every tongue confess that Messiah Jesus is Lord (see Phil. 2:10-11).

The Perfect Priest

For unlike the Old Covenant High Priest, Jesus lives forever. *Since He lives forever, He is always there to remind God the Father that He has paid for our sins with His own blood.* Therefore, He is exactly the kind of High Priest we need. He is not going to have a heart attack. He's not going to die and have to be replaced. For God the Father has given Him the place of glory and honor in heaven.

Jesus now ministers before God the Father as the holy and righteous representative of all His covenant children. He constantly bears our name on His shoulders and over His heart in the very throne room of God. He ministers there on our behalf as the perfect mediator we need. Therefore, we can do all things through Him who strengthens us (see Phil. 4:13). We confess our sins in His name and know He has forgiven us (see 1 John 1:9). Because our names are sealed on His shoulders and over His heart, He is able to keep us from falling and present us faultless before the presence of His glory with exceeding joy (see Jude 24). God accepts us in our High Priest.

Therefore, when Jesus died, the veil in the Temple that hid the glory of God from the face of the people was split down the middle. You see, it was no longer needed because the New Covenant had been cut at the cross. Jesus, through His blood, has carried us to "Father's house." Now we all may walk right into the heavenly Holy of Holies by the blood of Jesus. We may pray directly to the Father, in the name of the Son, through the Holy Spirit.

All believers in the Lord Jesus are now ministering priests of the Most High God. Speaking of this priesthood of the believer,

Peter writes, "But you are a chosen race, a royal priesthood, a holy nation, God's own people, that you may declare the wonderful deeds of him who called you out of darkness into his marvelous light" (1 Peter 2:9 RSV).

The High Priest on the Throne

When Jesus sprinkled His blood on the Mercy Seat, He did something that the Old Covenant High Priest could not do. *He sat down on the throne.* (See Ephesians 1:20; Revelation 3:21; 21:5; Acts 2:30.) The High Priest is on the throne because His work is complete. Looking ahead to this time, the prophet Zechariah wrote, "He shall build the temple of the Lord, and He shall fill it with splendor; He shall sit and rule upon His throne, and He shall be priest on His throne, and a perfect union will reign between the two (offices)" (Zech. 6:13 MLB).

Just as sure as the Mercy Seat was on the Ark of the Covenant, Jesus is on the throne of God. There He represents us before God the Father. He is the High Priest of all who have personally accepted Him as their sin offering.

All humanity must stand before God in the heavenly court-room of eternity. And the only evidence presented for the will to be executed is the blood of Jesus. If you have appropriated His blood, He will be your advocate before God the Father. The blood of Jesus will cry out on your behalf, "holiness unto the Lord." *You will be accepted in your righteous High Priest.*

Then shall the King say unto you, "…Come, ye blessed of my Father, inherit the kingdom prepared for you from the foundation of the world" (Matt. 25:34 KJV).

However, if you are not covered by His blood sacrifice, Jesus cannot represent you as your High Priest. The will cannot be executed. The verdict will be guilty. You will stand before God in the *Great White Throne Judgment.*

John had a vision of this judgment. He said,

> *And I saw the dead, small and great, stand before God; and the books were opened; and another book was opened which was the book of life; and the dead were judged out of those things which were written in the books, according to their works.*
>
> *And the sea gave up the dead which were in it; and death and hell [hades] delivered up the dead which were in them: and they were judged every man according to their works. And death and hell [hades] were cast into the lake of fire. This is the second death. And whosoever was not found written in the book of life was cast into the lake of fire* (Revelation 20:12-15 KJV).

These are the people who always said they were good enough to approach God on their own good works. They claimed they didn't need all that "blood business." God judges them on their own good works just as they desired. But they are cast into the lake of fire because their works of self-righteousness cannot cry out on their behalf, "holiness unto the Lord." This is not God's desire but He will not violate our free will. We determine our own destiny.

The High Priest Is Coming

As we see men's hearts failing for fear, as we see apostasy in the Church, as we see violence on a worldwide scale, as we see earthquakes on the increase, as we see an increase in the occult, as we see a one-world dictator, a one-world economy, a one-world religion, as we see a restored Jerusalem, so shall we soon see our great High Priest coming from the heavenly Holy of Holies as King of Kings and Lord of Lords.

Like the jingling bells of the Old Covenant priest, if we listen carefully, we can almost hear the footsteps of Jesus in Jerusalem. Even so, Lord Jesus, come.

What about you, dear reader? Are you trying to approach God by your own good works? You will never make it, you know. But forgiveness and reconciliation to God is available through the blood of Jesus. He's already taken your Certificate of Debt. And now He desires to represent you before God the Father. Embrace Him as Lord of your life.

Chapter 7

THE PASSOVER

Background

We come now to the Passover chapter of the blood covenant story. The setting is in the land of Goshen in northern Egypt. Abraham's descendants have been living there for 400 years. (see Genesis 15:13.) When they first went to Egypt, they were a family of 70 (see Exod. 1:5). But now they have grown to a nation of several million. Their number is as the stars in the sky and the sands upon the sea shore, just as God had promised Abraham (see Gen. 22:17).

In fact, there are so many Hebrews that Pharaoh, the king of Egypt, feels threatened by them. So he makes slaves of them and forces them into cruel and inhumane labor, treating them more like animals than human beings.

As time passes, the brutal taskmasters of Pharaoh are more than the Hebrews can bear. Finally in their misery and despair, they cry out to God to deliver them. God hears their groaning and He remembers His covenant with Abraham. (see Exodus 2:23-24.) God must deliver them from bondage and bring them into the land as He promised Abraham (see Gen. 13:15).

God chooses Moses as His instrument to lead the Hebrews out of bondage. Working through Moses, God sends ten terrible plagues against the gods of Egypt. This is God's way of getting Pharaoh to let the Hebrews go. But each time God sends a new plague, Pharaoh's heart hardens. (see Exodus 3-10.)

God has given Pharaoh every chance to let the Hebrews go but Pharaoh won't yield. So God declares a tenth and final plague, which is to kill the firstborn of every family. (see Exodus 11.) But along with the decree of death, God gives specific instructions on how to be saved from this death. What He said is recorded in Exodus 12:1-14. Let's read it together.

The Old Covenant

The Lord said to Moses and Aaron in the land of Egypt, This month shall be for you the beginning of months; it shall be the first month of the year for you. Tell all the congregation of Israel that on the tenth day of this month they shall take every man a lamb according to their fathers' houses, a lamb for a household; and if the household is too small for a lamb, then a man and his neighbor next to his house shall take according to the number of persons; according to what each can eat you shall make your count for the lamb. Your lamb shall be without blemish, a male a year old; you shall take it from the sheep or from the goats; and you shall keep it until the fourteenth day of this month, when the whole assembly of the congregation of Israel shall kill their lambs in the evening. Then they shall take some of the blood, and put it on the two doorposts and the lintel of the houses in which they eat them. They shall eat the flesh that night, roasted; with unleavened bread and bitter herbs they shall eat it. Do not eat any of it raw or boiled with water, but roasted, its head with its legs and its inner parts. And you shall let none of it remain until the morning, anything that remains until the morning you shall burn.

In this manner you shall eat it: your loins girded, your sandals on your feet, and your staff in your hand; and you shall eat it in haste. It is the Lord's passover. For I will pass through the land of Egypt that night, and I will smite all the first-born in the land of Egypt, both man and beast; and on all the gods of Egypt I will execute judgments: I am the Lord. The blood shall be a sign for you, upon the houses where you are; and when I see the blood, I will pass over you, and no plague shall fall upon you to destroy you, when I smite the land of Egypt. This day shall be for you a memorial day, and you shall keep it as a feast to the Lord; throughout your generations you shall observe it as an ordinance forever (Exodus 12:1-14 RSV).

Deliverance Instructions

We see that God instructs every man to select for his household a lamb without spot or blemish. He is to select this lamb on the *10th day* of the month. Then he is to observe this lamb for five days to make sure there is nothing wrong with him. There can be *no fault* (spot or blemish) found in this lamb.

On the *14th day* of the month, he is to bring the lamb to his doorstep and kill him. As he kills the animal, he will catch the blood in the basin at the foot of the doorstep. Then he is to take a hyssop bush, dip it in the blood, and sprinkle the blood on both sides of the doorpost and above the doorpost. There will be blood at the foot of the door, blood on both sides of the door, and blood at the top of the door. Thus, the entire entrance into the house will be covered by blood.

This is to be done on the evening of the 14th. Now the Hebrew day begins around 6 o'clock in the evening. So they had to kill the lambs around 3 o'clock in the afternoon of the 14th in order to eat the meal by 6 o'clock. So when 3 o'clock arrives, Hebrew knives flash against the Egyptian sun, as the lambs are killed and the blood is applied. The family then enters their house through the bloodstained door. Safe inside, they roast the lamb and eat it as they wait for the final plague of death to move through the land.

A National Cookout

Now this is no small town affair. There are literally tens of thousands of people killing lambs, sprinkling the blood on the doorposts, and going inside to roast the lambs. And they are all doing it at the same time.

You can imagine that the land of Goshen smelled like one great big lamb cookout. Think what it would be like today, if all the citizens of a city of two million residents went in their backyard at the same time and grilled steaks. Why you could smell those steaks and see that smoke for miles and miles.

That's what is happening with the Hebrews. You would smell those lambs being roasted all over Egypt. As the scent of the smoke ascended up into the heavens, it reached the very nostrils of God. *It was the evidence to God that the blood, representing the covenant relationship with Abraham's descendants, had been applied.* And now the covenant meal was being consumed to celebrate the communion of that covenant.

No Leftovers

In preparing the meal, *not one bone* of the lamb was to be broken (Exodus 12:46). And the whole lamb was to be consumed. *Nothing could be left over for the next day.* Anything the family couldn't eat was to be burned immediately.

Along with the lamb, the family also ate bitter herbs and unleavened bread. The bitter herbs were to remind them of their bitter times in bondage under Pharaoh. The unleavened bread would remind them they were eating on the run and didn't have time to properly prepare the bread. They ate the meal fully clothed with staff in hand ready to depart.

The Blood Covering

Although the family was inside the house and couldn't see the blood covering, they had faith that God would save them because of it. As they ate their meal, God allowed the angel of death to sweep through the land. As he passed from door to door he sought to enter every household. If the entrance was covered by blood the angel of death could not get in but had to pass over that house. The blood was a seal protecting the people inside. However, if the entrance was not covered by blood, judgment would come upon that household as the firstborn died.

In ancient times, people made sacrifices to their gods at the door of the dwelling. In fact, the entrance to a person's home was the earliest altar of ancient people. When they stepped over the threshold, they came under the protection of their household god. Because the Hebrews applied the blood to the entrance to the house, this blood covenant was also known as a "threshold covenant." When the people stepped over the threshold, they came under the protection of their covenant God. We will learn more about the Threshold Covenant in the next chapter.

A Lamb Defeats a Serpent

This was the Lord's Passover. And we see that He used the *blood of the lamb* as the means for bringing His people out of bondage to Egypt.

Now the symbol of Egypt was the serpent. In the Bible, the serpent represents satan (Rev. 12:9). What God is saying with this exodus is that in His own appointed time, *He will use the blood of the lamb to destroy satan's power and set people free from bondage to him.*

We learned in Chapter 5 that this has always been God's plan, even from the beginning. When satan was in the Garden of Eden, he introduced sin into the lives of God's creation. At that time God put a curse on satan. Genesis 3:15 is the key passage. God says to satan who appears as a serpent, "And I will put enmity between thee [satan] and the woman, and between thy seed and her seed; it [the woman's seed] shall bruise thy head and thou shalt bruise his heel" (KJV).

In this statement, God is saying that there will be two spiritual seeds or families in the world. One family will be the spiritual seed of satan. Satan is the spiritual father of all people who follow their own evil ways and seek only to gratify their own selfish desires and pleasures. They love the things of this world and the praise of men more than God. They worship at the shrine of intellect, materialism, pride, lust, and self-gratification. They reject the truth of God as revealed in Jesus Christ. Their rejection is manifested by either ignoring God's truth or seeking to destroy it. (see Ephesians 2:3; John 8:44.)

These are the spiritual children of satan. Satan's family began with Cain and has continued through his descendants whom satan used to establish his world system that we live in. It is a system of antichrist.

But God says there will also be a *seed of woman*. And God says the seed of woman will be a "He." Well, this is a curious phrase from God, because in the natural reproduction process, we are produced from the seed of man, not the seed of woman. Surely since God created us He knows how we reproduce each other. So He must have something special in mind. We'll see what it is later.

Then God says there will be constant war between the seed of the serpent, who is satan, and the seed of the woman. This continuous war will eventually come down to a personal confrontation between the two.

Satan will bruise the heel of the seed of the woman. This means he will strike him, wound him, bruise him, and afflict him. He will be brought like a lamb to the slaughter. He will be mocked at and sneered at. His strength will be poured out like water. His bones will be out of joint. His heart will melt like wax. His strength will dry up like sun-baked clay. His tongue will stick to his mouth. His bones will protrude out of his body. His hands and feet will be pierced. He will be sheared like a lamb at the slaughterhouse. His heel will be bruised.

Yet the seed of the woman will prevail. He will bruise the head of the serpent. Whereas a bruise to the heel is painful, a bruise to the head is fatal. This bruise to the head will destroy the serpent. Then the war will be over and the victory won. *The lamb will have defeated the serpent.*

A Nation Full of Lamb

As the Hebrew nation walked out of Egypt, each family had in them a whole lamb. *Every individual family member had feasted on the same lamb and he was in each of them.* Now we've learned that when the Hebrews offered up the blood of the lamb to God, they believed they were symbolically offering their own life to God. They knew that the life of the flesh was in the blood.

But the Hebrews had to have an altar where they could offer their sacrifice. In this time of deliverance from Egypt, the blood-sprinkled doorpost served as their altar. The lamb just took their place.

Since God told them to offer the lamb, it was an acceptable substitute for the entire nation. The blood offering would bring them into union with God. And as they ate the flesh of the sacrifice they symbolically would become one with God. This is the essence of the blood covenant as we learned in Chapter 2.

So the Hebrews believed that as they ate the sacrifice from which the blood was offered, they were symbolically feeding on and receiving into themselves the very life of God. This was communion between humans and God. Now there were many lambs sacrificed. But in the people's minds, as they ate the lambs, it was the one life of God coming into them and them into God. *Although they were from 12 different tribes, they were all part of the same lamb.* And so the entire nation had the "Lamb of God" in them as they were delivered from the bondage of the serpent.

The Covenant Meal

God established the Passover meal as an ordinance to be kept year after year, from generation to generation. This would be an everlasting memorial to their deliverance from bondage in Egypt. It was to be the communion meal to remind them that they were in an eternal covenant and union with God and with each other that could not be broken.

A House Cleaning

Now before the Passover celebration could begin, all the *leaven was to be removed* from the Hebrew's house. The leaven represented their old life of bondage in Egypt. So they were to purge out or remove the leaven from the house before they could have the covenant meal. In other words, they couldn't have leaven in the house while at the same time commune with God.

So before partaking of the meal, the head of the house would take a lighted candle and diligently search through every nook and cranny of the house looking for any hidden leaven. If he found any, he would immediately remove it from the house. Then the family would be ready for communion with God.

The modern Hebrew family participates in the same Passover house cleaning. Just before Passover, crumbs of unleavened bread are placed in each room of the house by one member of the family. Then the father proceeds from room to room looking for the hidden leaven. The family member goes along carrying a lighted candle to expose where the leaven is hidden. When the father finds the leaven, he is very careful not to touch it. He takes a feather and brushes it into a small wooden spoon. After he finds all the leaven, he puts the wooden spoon, the feather, and the candle in a cloth bound by string and burns it. With the leaven now purged from their household, they are ready to have communion with God through the covenant meal.

Partaking of the Meal

The family reclines at the table seated in order around the head of the house. The head of the house is responsible for explaining the meaning of the Passover to the children. When they ask the meaning, he replies, "It is the sacrifice of the Lord's Passover, who passed over the houses of the children of Israel in Egypt, when he smote the Egyptians, and delivered our houses." (see Exodus 12:27 KJV.) Jewish people today go through this same ceremony with some variations.

The Cup

Now when God renewed His covenant with Abraham, He made Abraham three promises. One promise was that Abraham would have so *many descendants*, that their number would be as the stars in the sky and the sands upon the sea shore. Another was that Abraham's descendants would *possess the land* God had given to Abraham. The third promise was that *one would come* as a descendant of Abraham who would be a blessing to the whole world. This is the seed (singular) of Abraham we have learned about in the previous chapters of this book. *The "coming one" would not only be their king, but somehow in a way they didn't fully understand, He would be "God living among them."* He would be their God and they would be His people. (see Genesis 12:1-3; 13:15-16; 15:18; 17:1-8.)

After the Hebrews possessed their promised land and became a great nation, they began to look for the fulfillment of this third promise. They began to look for the "coming one." *What better way could they anticipate his coming than by setting aside a place for him at the Passover meal which symbolized their communion with God.* And this they did. They began placing a cup at the end of the table. It was called "the cup" or "the cup of blessing" (see 1 Cor. 10:16). No one could drink from "the cup" because it was reserved for the "coming one." According to tradition, when he came, he would drink of "the cup" and cut a new covenant with his people. So they left a place looking forward to this time.

They also set aside a cup for Elijah. They believed that Elijah would come and announce the coming of the king. (See Malachi 3:1; 4:5-6.) He would prepare the people to receive the "coming one." So at the beginning of the covenant meal, the youngest of the family would open the door and invite Elijah to come and join them in the meal. The entire family would stand and say, "Blessed is he that cometh." But he does not come. So the youngest returns to his place at the table.

Then they recite the following prayer: "How long, O Lord, how long wilt thy anger not be turned away from thy people Israel and wilt thou have mercy and restore us again to thy favor? Behold our sufferings: we are scattered among the heathen and they mock us saying: where is thy God, and where is the promise of His coming? We grow faint, yet we hope."

The Bread

Instead of putting unleavened bread on the plate, they began to put it in a small bag embroidered with gold thread. This bag had three compartments. Three pieces of unleavened bread, called matzah, were placed in the bag, one piece in each separate compartment. *During the meal, the host would take out the middle piece of matzah, break it, and pass it around the table.* Each member would then break off a piece and eat it.

The Jewish people believed that these three pieces of bread represented their forefathers; Abraham, Isaac, and Jacob. They broke the middle piece to symbolize Isaac being offered as a sacrifice. But they didn't quite understand this interpretation because Isaac was not really sacrificed. Even today, they can't satisfactorily explain it.

The middle piece of *matzah* that was broken, passed around and was eaten, was called the afikomen. The word *afikomen* is derived from the Greek word *aperchomenos*, which means the "coming one."

Temple Passover

Later when the Temple was built, instead of killing the lambs at the doorpost, the people would bring the lambs to Jerusalem and kill them at the Temple.

The Passover celebration was a time of great joy, praise and adoration in worship to God. As they sacrificed at the Temple, the Levites would lead the people in singing the Psalms of David. They specifically sang Psalms 113-118. They begin with everyone singing the first line of each Psalm. Then the Levites would sing the second line of each Psalm and the people would respond by saying "Hallelujah" or "Praise the Lord.'

The singing was accompanied with musical instruments of trumpets, harps, flutes, tambourines, the cymbals, and other instruments. It reached its peak as the entire nation lifted their voices to God and sang, "This is the day the Lord has made; we will rejoice and be glad in it." (see Psalm 118:24.)

One Passover, during the reign of King Hezekiah, was such a wonderful festival of praise, that they continued it for seven more days. (See First Chronicles 30:23-24.) It was like bringing God back for an encore. Later, King Josiah, not to be outdone, personally contributed 30,000 animals for sacrifice (see 2 Chronicles 35:7). So Passover was a time of great joy and celebration.

Temple Lambs

As time passed; however, it became more difficult for the people in the outlying areas to bring their sacrifice to Jerusalem. So the Levites begin raising lambs for the Passover sacrifice right in Jerusalem and selling them at the Temple.

In this way, when the Jews came to Jerusalem to celebrate Passover, they could buy a lamb already set aside for sacrifice. It would be a lamb that had been closely inspected and without spot or blemish. It was a lamb in which they found no fault but it was born to die as a Passover lamb.

Arriving for Passover

Put yourself in this scene and come along with me now to Jerusalem to celebrate Passover. It's always exciting to go to

Jerusalem. I have been there myself about thirty times. This is the city of your God. And as you arrive on the outskirts of town, the majesty of the Temple dominates the city. All eyes are fixed on it, as the masses of people crowd into the Temple area.

Somehow, in the midst of all the bumping, crowding, and pushing, you make your way to purchase a lamb. You overheard someone say there are about 250,000 Passover lambs this year. (Josephus, a first-century Jewish historian reported there were about 256,500.) Your body trembles and your soul rejoices as the sounds of the hundreds of thousands of lambs waiting to be sacrificed fill the city. There is an excitement in the air as people anticipate the festival of praise.

It's not much time until 3 o'clock when the lambs are to be slaughtered. So you hurriedly make your way through the crowds and purchase your lamb. Then you move with the crowds toward the Altar at the Temple where the sacrifices will be made.

The Jerusalem Slaughter House

The Levites are lined up in two long rows stretching from the Altar way out to the people. Each Levite has a basin in his hand to catch the blood, just as the threshold caught the blood back in Egypt. The basin is pointed at the bottom to keep the Levite from setting it down, else the blood would congeal.

Finally the time everyone has been waiting for arrives. It is 3 o'clock. All you see is the flashing knives as the bloody animals are being slaughtered. As you cut the throat of your own lamb, the warm blood flows through your fingers. Although it is not like your pet lamb back home and is somewhat impersonal, still you can identify with the animal.

The Levite standing before you catches the blood in the basin. Quickly he passes it up the line to the Levite nearest the Altar. Very methodically, he takes the basin and throws the blood against the altar. Then he passes the empty basin back down the line of Levites to catch the blood of another lamb. And so you rejoice and sing the great Psalms of praise to God as you prepare for your Passover meal.

The New Covenant

For 1,500 years this Passover picture was pointing to a person. When it came time for the person to come, God sent forth His only Son who was born of the seed of woman. (see Galatians 4:4.) He was born of the seed of woman because He was brought into the world through the womb of a woman who had never known a man. He was born of a virgin. *God bypassed the natural reproduction process and prepared for Himself a body.* He was referred to as Emmanuel which means "God is with us." They called His name Jesus (Yeshua). (see Luke 1:27-31; Matthew 1:23.)

A prophet in the spirit of Elijah preceded Him to prepare the people to receive Jesus as the "coming one." It was prophesied that this forerunner to Jesus would turn many of Abraham's descendants to the Lord their God. (see Luke 1:16.) John the Baptist was that voice crying in the wilderness, "...Prepare the way of the Lord, make his paths straight." (see Luke 3:4 RSV.) He explained the meaning of these words as he preached, "Repent, for the kingdom of heaven has come near (arrived)" (Matthew 3:2 MLB). John was saying, "The King is coming. Get ready to receive Him."

Jesus said that John the Baptist was the one who would announce that the king is coming. (see Isaiah 40:3; Malachi 3:1;

4:5-6; Matthew 3:2; 17:10-12; 21:12; Mark 1:2; Luke 1:16-17; 7:27.) *But the king is introduced on the scene by John the Baptist as the "Lamb of God" who takes away the sin of the world* (see John 1:29).

Immediately after that proclamation, Jesus is driven into the wilderness to do battle with the serpent. But he returns in the power of the Spirit and His fame begins to spread throughout the region (see Luke 4:1-15).

Three years later on the 10th day of the month of Passover, which was exactly the same day the pet lambs were set aside back in Egypt, the real "Lamb of God" enters Jerusalem. The people take branches of palm trees and go out to meet Him. As He comes near, the people shout, "...Hosanna! Blessed is he who comes in the name of the Lord! Blessed is the King of Israel" (John 12:13 NIV).

Jesus, entering Jerusalem on a donkey, is fulfilling a 400-year-old prophecy by the prophet Zechariah. Zechariah was speaking of this occasion when he said, "Rejoice greatly, O daughter of Zion: shout O daughter of Jerusalem; behold thy King cometh unto thee; he is just, and having salvation; lowly, and riding upon an ass, and upon a colt the foal of an ass" (Zechariah 9:9 KJV). (see John 12:1-5.)

Yet still the seed of the serpent, certain religious and political leaders, the establishment, seek to kill Him. For five days they observe and test Him. But there's nothing wrong with Him. He is spotless and without blemish. *They can find no fault in Him because He was born to die as a Passover lamb.*

So as Passover begins on the evening of the 14th, Jesus is careful not to be seen around the Temple. He sends two of His disciples, Peter and John, into the city. They are to find a certain man who has purchased a lamb and prepared a room for them where they can safely have their Passover meal together (see Luke 22:1-13). They had a private Passover in anticipation of the national celebration that would take place later the next afternoon.

Jesus, as the head of the group, explains the meaning of the Passover. No doubt He leads them in singing, "This is the day the Lord has made, let us rejoice and be glad in it."

The New Covenant Meal

As an observant Jew, Jesus gave the traditional Jewish blessing over the bread, "Blessed are You, O Lord our God, King of the universe, who brings forth bread from the earth." The Hebrew is *"Barukh atah Adonai Elohenu melekh ha-olam, ha-motzee lekhem meen ha-aretz."*

At the end of the meal, Jesus makes an unusual move. He picks up the bag with the bread in it and pulls out the middle piece. Then Jesus breaks the middle piece, gives it to His disciples and says, "...This is my body given for you; do this in remembrance of me" (Luke 22:19 NIV).

It's not Abraham, Isaac, and Jacob after all. It's Father, Son, and Holy Spirit. You see, the middle piece didn't look back to Isaac who needed a substitute. It looked ahead to Jesus, the real "Lamb of God" who was to give Himself. *Jesus is the reality of that broken matzah.*

Jesus then gave the blessing over the wine, "Blessed are You, O Lord our God, King of the universe, who creates the fruit of the vine." The Hebrew is *"Barukh atah Adonai Elohenu melekh ha-olam, boray p'ree ha-gahfen."*

Then Jesus took "the cup," gave it to His disciples and said, "...All of you drink of it; for this is My blood of the new covenant poured out for man for the forgiveness of sins." (see Matthew 26:27-28 MLB.) Then Jesus said, "I tell you I shall not drink again of this fruit of the vine until that day when I drink it new with you in My Father's kingdom." (see Matthew 26:29 RSV.)

With these words Jesus was saying, "Men everywhere long for life. They seek union with God. They give of their own blood or the blood of a substitute. Then they drink the blood or the blood of the grapes as a substitute to express this desire. They eat the flesh of the sacrifice to express their desire for communion with God. All that man reaches out for, I supply. In Me is life. I am the 'Coming One' you've been waiting for and anticipating. If you will partake of My life, you will partake of the life of God. This is the new covenant in My blood."

The Lamb on the Cross

Then Jesus went out and had a personal confrontation with satan. At 9 o'clock that Passover morning as the lambs were being prepared for sacrifice, Jesus was nailed to the cross (see Mark 15:25). (The third hour was 9 o'clock in the morning, Jewish time.)

On the crucifixion tree, Jesus bore our sins and carried our sorrows. He was wounded for our transgressions. He was bruised for our iniquities. God laid on Him the iniquity of us all. He was oppressed and afflicted. Yet, He opened not His mouth, like a lamb led to the slaughter.

His strength was poured out like water. His bones were out of joint. His heart melted like wax. His strength dried up like sun-baked clay. His tongue stuck to His mouth. His boned protruded out of His body. He was sheared like a lamb at the slaughter house. His heel was bruised. (see Isaiah 53; Psalm 22:14-27).

These are prophecies describing Jesus' crucifixion. You see, when a person is crucified, his body sags. So he pushes himself up by his heel to get more air into his lungs. This act of pushing bruises his heel.

At 3 o'clock when the people are singing praises to God that echo throughout the hills of Jerusalem, the lambs are slaughtered. As that same moment, as the shouts of "Hallelujah" and "Praise the Lord" ring out on the hill known today as the Temple Mount, Jesus died. Like the picture on the doorpost centuries earlier in Egypt, the blood of Jesus, the human Lamb of God covered the cross.

To perfectly complete the picture, *not one bone of this Lamb of God was broken*. (see Exodus 12:46; Psalm 34:20; John 19:36.) And the *entire lamb* was consumed being roasted by the judgment fires of God as He became our sin substitute.

Jeremiah wrote of this time and said that God would send fire into His bones and consume the entire sacrifice (see Lam. 1:13). And the Jewish establishment, not knowing they were further fulfilling prophecy, hurriedly took His body down before 6 o'clock, so that there would be *nothing of Him left over* (left on the cross for the next day (see Exod. 12:10; John 19:31).

Blood and Water

I mentioned that the Hebrews in Egypt used a hyssop bush to sprinkle the blood of the lamb on the doorpost. The hyssop bush holds water in its stem. When the blood was applied, water would flow out of the stem and cover the blood. The entire entrance into the house was covered with blood and water.

We learned in Chapter 4 that when Moses received the Ten Commandments, he took a hyssop bush, dipped it into blood, and sprinkled it over the stone tables and towards all the people. Later, he sprinkled blood over the tabernacle and all its furnishings used in worship as well as the priest. They were all sealed with blood and water.

Then in order to enter the tabernacle and approach God, the High Priest has to go by way of the blood at the Altar and the water at the Laver. From there he carried the name of each of the 12 tribes sealed in stone over his heart and on his shoulders.

Later when the Temple was built, blood drained into basins underneath the Altar. Water flowed through these basins carrying the blood outside the Temple so that the people could see that their sacrifice had been accepted. They saw the blood and water. When Jesus was crucified, they pierced Him in the side and out flowed blood and water (see John 19:34). All of these sacrifices were pictures pointing to Him as our Passover lamb (see 1 Cor. 5:7).

The blood represents a life given while the water represents a life received. Jesus gave His life for us at the Cross. There His blood was poured out on our behalf. But we get no benefit from Him giving His life unless we personally receive it for ourselves. You see, the blood of Jesus alone will not save you unless you appropriate it for your own life.

And you appropriate it for your own life by asking Him to come into your life and be your Savior. You accept Him into your heart as the "Lamb of God" who died for your sins. *Jesus then comes into your life through the person of the Holy Spirit. This is the meaning of the water that sealed every place where the blood was applied.* It looked forward to us receiving the Holy Spirit. Whoever applies the blood of Jesus to their life is sealed with the Holy Spirit. (see Ephesians 1:13; 4:30; 2 Corinthians 1:22; 1 Peter 1:5.)

At the Feast of Tabernacles, when water was being poured into the basin at the foot of the Altar, Jesus stood and said,

> ...*If any one thirst, let him come to me and drink. He who believes in me, as the scripture has said, 'Out of his heart shall flow rivers of living water.' Now this he said about the Spirit, which those who believed in him were to receive; for as yet the Spirit had not been given, because Jesus was not yet glorified* (John 7:38-39 RSV).

But now Jesus is glorified. And whoever drinks of the waters of the Holy Spirit shall never thirst again. The Holy Spirit shall become within him a well of water springing up to everlasting life (see John 4:13-14).

It's a Celebration

This is what the New Covenant meal is all about. When we partake of it, we are not just remembering a life given; we are celebrating a *life received.* It is God's life, and we have received it. This is why communion is to be a time of great joy, and praise, and worship.

Most communion services I've been to remind me of a funeral home. Everybody wears a long face and will hardly breathe lest their gasping for breath break the silence and offend God. We unwittingly have believed this "holy hush" is pleasing to God. Well, that's okay if your God is dead.

But mine isn't! The cross is bare! The tomb is empty! *Jesus is alive!* He publicly destroyed satan at the Cross where He purchased our salvation. (See Colossians 2:15.) The blood of the lamb destroyed the serpent and set us free from bondage to him. Death cannot enter the heart of one who is covered with the blood of Jesus and sealed with the Holy Spirit. Death is swallowed up in victory. God has given us the victory through Jesus Christ our Lord (see 1 Cor. 15:54-58). The war is over. *We've won!*

God the Father has...

> *...raised Christ [Messiah] from the dead and seated him in the place of honor at God's right hand in heaven, far, far, above any other king or ruler or dictator or leader. Yes, his honor is far more glorious than that of anyone else either in this world or in the world to come. And God has put all things under his feet and made him the supreme Head of the church—which is his body, filled with himself, the Author and Giver of everything everywhere* (Ephesians 1:20-23 TLB).

The seed of the woman bruised the head of the serpent through His resurrection.

And now we have received that same life in us. We too have victory over satan for greater is He who is in us than He who is in the world (see 1 John 4:4).

The Lamb on the Throne

In the Book of Revelation, John stood before one on the throne who had a scroll with writing on the inside and the back. It was sealed with seven seals. John heard a mighty angel with a loud voice saying, "Who is worthy to open the book and loose the seals?" No one in Heaven, nor in earth, nor under the earth was able to open the book. No one could even look upon it. Then John wept for no one was found worthy to open and read the book, neither to look upon it.

One of the elders before the throne said unto John, "Weep not. Look, the Lion of the tribe of Judah, the Root of David, has prevailed to open the book." As John turned to see this *Lion,* he saw standing in the center of the Throne, a *Lamb* as it had been slain. The Greek word John chose to refer to this lamb is *arnios.* It means a little, "pet lamb." Just like back in Egypt.

And when the Lamb took the book, those around the throne fell down at His feet and sung a new song saying, "Thou art worthy to take the book and to open the seals thereof: for thou wast slain, and hast redeemed us to God by thy blood out of every kindred, and tongue, and people, and nation; and hast made us unto our God kings and priests: and we shall reign on the earth."

Then John saw and heard the voice of many angels around the throne and all that were there numbered ten thousand times ten thousand, and thousands of thousands saying with a loud voice, "Worthy is the Lamb that was slain to receive power, and riches, and wisdom, and strength, and honor, and glory, and blessing." And John heard every creature in heaven, and on the earth, and in the sea say, "Blessing and honor, and glory, and power be unto Him that sits on the throne, and unto the Lamb forever and ever." (see Revelation 5.)

The King Is Coming

All who know Jesus as their Messiah and Lord and Savior drink of the fruit of the vine in remembrance of His life given for us and to us. As we partake of the covenant meal, we look forward to the time when we will partake of it with our heavenly Father at the "marriage supper of the Lamb." (see Revelation 19:1-9.) It will be a time of great joy and praise and worship to God echoing throughout the hills of the New Jerusalem. And instead of being on Mount Calvary it will be on Mount Zion where Jesus, the "Lamb of God," will reign as King of Kings and Lord of Lords (Psalms 2:6-8; 48:1-2). There we shall reign with Him as kings and priests of the Most High God.

The Jewish people complete their Passover service by saying, *L'Shanah Haba-ah, Bi-yerushala-yim,* which means "next year in Jerusalem." So we partake of the covenant meal by saying, "next year at the marriage supper of the Lamb." Hallelujah! *The king is coming.*

The Covenant Terms

Before partaking of the covenant meal, it is good to be reminded of the terms of the covenant. When we hear them, it fills our hearts with songs of joy and gladness such that sorrow and mourning shall flee away. (see Isaiah 35:10; 51:11.)

Here are the terms. God says to His people,

> *For I will take you from among the heathen, and gather you out of all countries, and will bring you into your own land. Then will I sprinkle clean water upon you, and ye shall be clean: from all your filthiness, and from all your idols, will I cleanse you. A new heart also will I give you: and I will take away the stony heart out of your flesh, and I will give you an heart of flesh. And I will put my spirit within you, and cause you to walk in my statutes, and ye shall keep my judgments and do them. And ye shall dwell in the land that I gave to your fathers; and ye shall be my people, and I will be your God* (Ezekiel 36:24-28 KJV).

And then in Hebrews 8:10-12 God says,

For this is the covenant that I will make with the house of Israel after those days, saith the Lord; I will put my laws into their mind and write them in their hearts: and I will be to them a God, and they shall be to me a people: And they shall not teach every man his neighbor, and every man his brother, saying, Know the Lord: for all shall know me, from the least to the greatest. For I will be merciful to their unrighteousness and their sins and their iniquities will I remember no more (Hebrews 8:10-12 KJV).

There Is Only One Lamb

Believers know God because the Holy Spirit within us bears witness to our human spirit that we are children of God by faith in Jesus (see Rom. 8:15-16; Gal. 3:26). *The "Lamb of God" has come to live in each of us in the person of the Holy Spirit.*

Although we, like the Jewish people, may come from different denominational tribes, we are all part of the same "Lamb of God." There is no Catholic and Protestant "Lamb of God." Neither is there a Baptist, Methodist, Lutheran, Pentecostal, Presbyterian, etc., "Lamb of God." There is only one "Lamb of God." *And He is in each of us who have received Jesus into our heart.*

We're not in covenant with an organization; we are in covenant with a person. Our faith is not in a religion but in a relationship with the Almighty through Jesus. He is the basis for our fellowship. Paul reminds us of this by saying, "The cup of blessing which we bless, is it not the communion of the blood of Christ [Messiah]? The bread which we break, is it not the communion of the body of Christ [Messiah]? For we being many are one bread, and one body: for we are all partakers of that one bread." (See

1 Corinthians 10:16-17 KJV.) Therefore, all who know Jesus are welcome to share in the covenant meal. All may feed at the table of communion.

A Spiritual House Cleaning

Remember the Hebrew had to purge out the leaven from his house before he could eat the communion meal. Well, in the Bible, leaven represents sin. And believers are now the spiritual house of God. Our body is the Temple of the Holy Spirit. (see 1 Corinthians 3:16; 6:19-20.)

So, we too must take a lighted candle, which is the Holy Spirit, and let Him search through every nook and cranny of our spiritual house looking for any hidden leaven (sin) that would keep us from enjoying fellowship with our heavenly Father.

Paul puts it this way, "Purge out therefore the old leaven, that ye may be a new lump, as ye are unleavened. For even Christ [Messiah] our Passover is sacrificed for us: Therefore let us keep the feast, not with the old leaven, neither with the leaven of malice and wickedness; but with the unleavened bread of sincerity and truth" (1 Cor. 5:7-8 KJV).

He further says,

> *So if anyone eats this bread and drinks from this cup of the Lord in an unworthy manner, he is guilty of sin against the body and the blood of the Lord. That is why a man should examine himself carefully before eating the bread and drinking from the cup. For if he eats the bread and drinks from the cup unworthily, not thinking about the body of Christ [Messiah] and what it means, he is eating and drinking God's judgment upon himself; for he is trifling with the death of Christ*

[Messiah]. That is why many of you are weak and sick and some have even died (1 Corinthians 11:27-30 TLB).

As the head of the Hebrew household would not touch the exposed leaven, so God says to us, "...touch not the unclean thing; and I will receive you" (2 Corinthians 6:17 KJV). But instead of burning the leaven in a cloth, we let the fire of the Holy Spirit cleanse us.

The prayer we offer for spiritual cleansing is, "Search me, O God, and know my heart; try me and know my thoughts and see if there be any wicked way in me, and lead me in the way everlasting" (Ps. 139:23-24 KJV).

As the Holy Spirit cleanses us, He also assures us that, "If we confess our sins, he [God] is faithful and just to forgive us our sins, and to cleanse us from all unrighteousness" (1 John 1:9 KJV). "There is therefore now no condemnation for those who are in Christ [Messiah] Jesus" (Romans 8:1 RSV).

Yes, He loves you and wants to bless you. He wants you to enter into this glorious covenant with Him. If you still haven't done so, now is the time for your salvation. Ask Him now to come into your life. And may the grace of Jesus our Lord, the love of God our Father and the communion of the Holy Spirit be with you.

> *Now unto him that is able to keep you from falling, and to present you faultless before the presence of his glory with exceeding joy, To the only wise God our Savior be glory and majesty, dominion and power, both now and ever. Amen* (Jude 24-25 KJV).

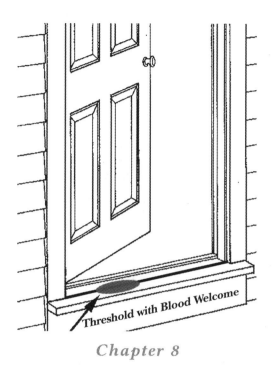

Threshold with Blood Welcome

Chapter 8

THE THRESHOLD COVENANT

There are many powerful concepts and teachings in the Bible that have been lost to us because of the cultural and historical differences in Bible times and our times. They don't necessarily affect our eternal salvation, but some of these are so foundational that they dramatically affect our understanding the Bible, the God of the Bible, and our walk with God.

God spoke to the people in their culture and used customs and traditions they were familiar with and understood. Western believers miss so much of the richness and depths of these stories because we are not familiar with the customs and practices. This is why it is so important to study and understand the Hebraic culture of the Bible. It is the root of our Christian faith that gives us a fresh and exciting revelation of Jesus who taught and lived in the culture of His own people.

One of the most powerful customs God used that we really need to discover is that of the "Threshold Covenant." An understanding of the Threshold Covenant and how it points to Jesus can literally transform our understanding of the Bible and our walk with God. This is a phrase most Christians have never heard. And that is the point.

In all of my years of studying the Bible and its culture, I was not familiar with the concept until I happened to find a book written by H. Clay Trumbull entitled *The Threshold Covenant.* This book was originally published in 1896. It is technical and not written for the general public. It was republished in 2000 by Impact Christian Books, Kirkwood, Missouri. As there is very little written on this subject, much of what I am explaining and the examples I am citing in this chapter are from his book. I have written it in clear, everyday language.

Let's begin with this understanding—the Threshold Covenant was perhaps the most important and powerful custom and practice of people in Bible times. It was the foundation on which primitive people built all of their relationships with the gods they worshiped and the people they knew. Unfortunately, it is a custom and practice that has been lost to us modern-day believers. An understanding of the Threshold Covenant will greatly enrich our understanding of the Bible, the God of the Bible, our walk with God, and our relationship with people. Because the Threshold Covenant is a variation of the blood covenant and Passover, I thought it important to add this chapter to *The Miracle of the Scarlet Thread*.

Reviewing Passover

In the previous chapter, we studied the Passover and how it was a picture of Jesus our Passover Lamb. We learned how God told the Hebrews to select a lamb on the tenth day of the month and observe the lamb for five days to make sure it was without spot or blemish. Then on the fourteenth day they were to kill the lamb between the evenings (3:00 p.m.).

They were to kill the lamb in such a way that they didn't break any bones in the lamb and they were to consume the entire sacrifice leaving nothing left over for the next day. They were to kill the lamb at the doorpost of their dwelling and put the blood of the lamb on their door. In essence, Passover was a Threshold or "Crossing Over" Covenant.

God told the people that He would pass through the land with His executioner who would execute judgment on the gods of Egypt by taking the life of the firstborn. People in Bible times were familiar with the sight of kings and emperors traveling through their empire with their executioners to judge their enemies. So this was language the people understood.

God said He would pass over (through) the dwellings where the blood had been applied and the people would be spared. However, if the blood was not applied death would come to the firstborn of the household.

In Bible times, it was a common belief that the first fruits of life belonged to the gods the people worshiped. This included the fields, the flocks, the herds, and the family. The God of the Bible confirmed this view when He said that the first fruits of our family and all our resources belong to Him.

In Egypt, the people accepted the idea that their gods had the rights to their firstborn. As such, the life and well-being of the firstborn represented the power and protection of the gods. If the gods could not protect the firstborn belonging to them, then their glory was diminished. The One True God was to challenge the gods of Egypt through the firstborn. By judging the firstborn of Egypt while protecting the firstborn of His own, the God of the Hebrews would establish Himself as the One True God.

Now let's read Exodus 12:21-23:

> *Then Moses called for all the elders of Israel and said to them, "Pick out and take lambs for yourselves according to your families, and kill the Passover lamb. And you shall take a bunch of hyssop, dip it in the blood that is in the basin, and strike the lintel [crosspiece at top of the door] and the two doorposts with the blood that is in the basin. And none of you shall go out of his house until morning. For the Lord will pass through to strike the Egyptians; and when He sees the blood on the lintel and on the two doorposts, the Lord will pass over [stand in] the door and not allow the destroyer to come into your houses to strike you."*

We see that Moses tells the people to dip the hyssop in the blood in the basin. The Hebrew word for basin is *saf*, which means "threshold." It was the threshold which was the bottom of the entrance to the door. Translating *saf* into English as *basin* can cause us to miss the core concept of the story. The people were

212

to dip in the blood on the threshold, on the two side posts of the door, and over the door.

Now here is an insight that is so powerful it is mind boggling. In doing this study, I was curious to learn more about the threshold as a picture of Jesus. I consulted the Browns, Driver, Briggs Hebrew-English Lexicon. This is a scholarly book explaining the meaning of words in the Bible. In Hebrew, the word for threshold is miphtan (pronounced miftawn). I was overwhelmed to learn that in Hebrew threshold means crossbeam and in Arabic it means carpenter. Did you get that? The blood stained threshold was a picture of a carpenter carrying a cross. Oh my, is our God amazing. He is the greatest painter of pictures of all time. What picture would He paint of my life, or your life?

The Hebrews understood that God was going to bring judgment on the gods of Egypt by taking the life of the firstborn. For them to be saved from this judgment, they made a blood sacrifice at the threshold of their door to welcome the One True God into their home to be their covenant God, provider, and protector.

Why would God have the Hebrews do this? Why would this be important? Why didn't He choose some other method of deliverance? What did this mean to them, if anything? Was this a custom they understood or was God giving them some new and strange ceremony? What was this all about? To understand why God did this the way He did it, we must understand the cultural and historical background to this story.

A Bloody Door Covenant

It all goes back to creation. When God made mankind in His image, He gave us a spirit that causes us to have a need to worship Him. Now think about it—the history of the human race is clear that human beings are worshipers. We are not whole beings unless we worship our Creator. And if we don't worship Him, we will worship someone else or some thing. That is why people adore sports heroes and celebrities in the music and entertainment industry. This is our human nature.

In the book of Genesis we learn that our first ancestors worshiped God by building altars and making sacrifices to Him. They understood that the life of the flesh is in the blood (see Leviticus 17:11), and by offering an innocent substitutionary blood sacrifice they were offering their own life to God in a sacred blood covenant. Later, as they turned away from their Creator, people worshiped false gods and demonic idols through blood sacrifices.

Now this is really important. In their study of the earliest historic records of the human race, researchers have discovered that man's earliest, most primitive altar to the One True God as well as false gods was the threshold or entrance way into the home. Primitive people worshiped at their bloody threshold door altar long before they built temples and other public worship structures.

Long before there was organized religion with formal priests, the father was the family priest. He was responsible to make sacrifices to the gods the family worshiped, and he did so at the entrance to the family's dwelling. The threshold of the door was the family's altar to their gods. The family made the threshold with a narrow groove or a round hole where they could pour the blood. They made a blood covenant sacrifice at the threshold as their way of requesting protection from the family deity as well as inviting the deity into their home.

By dedicating themselves and worshiping at the bloody threshold door altar, the family's gods were responsible to protect and provide for the family. Furthermore, when a guest was invited into the home, the host would kill an animal and offer its blood at the threshold as a means of making a sacred blood covenant with the guest.

Through the offering of the blood sacrifice, the guest came under the protection of the family deity as well as the host. Once the sacrifice was made, the guest would *step over* the blood-stained threshold and enter the home. To step on the threshold was to dishonor and despise the family's gods. The guest was then accepted by the deity and the host family as a covenant friend.

All the protection and provisions of the deity as well as those of the host family were extended to the honored guests. I experienced something similar when visiting an Arab family in Israel. While the father did not kill an animal, he spoke to me using covenant terms and made it clear that as long as I was in his home I was under his protection and his provisions were mine.

To summarize, it was the common practice to kill an animal at the threshold of the home as the way of welcoming the family deity as well as honored guests. When the guests crossed the bloody threshold and entered the house through the door, they were entitled to the protection and provisions of the household as a covenant right.

If an honored guest arrived unexpectedly and there was no time to prepare the sacrifice, the host would sprinkle salt on the threshold. In ancient times, salt represented blood and was often used as a substitute for blood. It still is today. I explain this in the next chapter on the Salt Covenant.

Examples of the Threshold Covenant

Because Western nations are relatively new in history, we look to more ancient civilizations for evidences of Threshold Covenant customs and practices. For example, in African, Middle Eastern, and Asian countries guests were welcomed by the host family killing an animal and putting its blood on the threshold of the door or entrance way into the home. *To step over the threshold was to accept the covenant offered by the family. To trample underfoot the blood was to show contempt and rejection of the covenant. This was the greatest of insults in ancient times.*

Furthermore, if someone entered the home any way except by crossing over the bloodstained threshold, it meant they were an enemy who came to steal, kill, and destroy. The protection and provisions of the household were not afforded to them as there was no blood covenant with the host family and their gods.

Ancient Egyptians, such as those during the Passover story, worshiped the false deity called Osiris. As was common in worship, they had an annual feast in honor of Osiris. As part of their worship, they sacrificed an animal to Osiris before the door of their house on the evening before the festival. To the Egyptians, Osiris was the judge of the soul after death. They wanted to live with Osiris in the afterlife, so they offered a sacrifice to welcome Osiris into their home. Osiris was then responsible to protect them from the finality of death and give them victory over death. The blood poured out at the doorpost was the act of making covenant with Osiris who would protect them and provide safe passage through evil forces in the afterlife.

There are numerous examples of the threshold covenant in more modern times. In the 1880s in Egypt, when a new ruler came to his palace, a threshold sacrifice was offered to welcome him. At the gate entrance to his palace, animals were slaughtered in his honor. The blood of the animals was splashed across the threshold at the gate so that the horses' hoofs and wheels of the carriage passed through it. In this way, the ruler and the people were in blood covenant with each other. The ruler was responsible for the protection of the people and they were responsible to honor and obey the ruler.

In 1878, Civil War general and former president Ulysses S. Grant and his family arrived in Egypt on a tour. At his arrival, a bull was sacrificed where his ship docked. The blood of the animal was splashed under the gangplank so that Grant crossed over it in stepping from the ship to the shore.

When Grant reached the house of his host, a sheep was sacrificed at the threshold so that Grant crossed over or passed over the blood when he entered the house. This was a threshold blood covenant sacrifice offering friendship between Egypt and the former president and general.

Once again, Egypt provided us with a powerful example of the Threshold Covenant. When someone bought a boat, an animal was killed and the blood sprinkled at the gangplank so that the owner would have to cross over the blood before entering the threshold of the boat. *This is the origin of the modern custom of "christening" a ship at the time of its launching.*

Participants break a bottle of wine, "the blood of the grapes," on the bow of the ship before it crosses the threshold of the deep water into the sea. Without knowing the background of the custom nor what they are really doing, the people are make a threshold blood covenant with God seeking His protection over the ship, its crew, and its passengers.

The Sacredness of the Threshold Altar

Because the threshold was the family altar and the place of the sacrificial blood of a covenant, it was considered sacred and not to be stepped on. Family members and guests were to cross over it with great reverence and respect. It was considered a bad omen if one accidentally struck his or her foot on the threshold. To honor or dishonor the threshold was to honor or dishonor the protecting deity of the home as well as the hosts.

Because the threshold was the sacred altar of worship, people placed images of their gods underneath it as a way of guarding the entrance into the house against evil spirits. On the Big Island of Hawaii, I have seen images made by early inhabitants representing their gods facing the ocean to protect the villagers from invaders from the sea.

People placed charms on their doors to ward off evil spirits. Primitive people believed that evil spirits would not pass through iron. As a result, they would attach iron images and charms to the doors to prevent spirits from entering the house. This is the origin of the modern custom of putting horseshoes on the doors of homes as good luck charms.

When I was a boy my family had a horseshoe attached to the front door. I clearly remember we all participated in nailing it to the door. Many people did this. We didn't know anything about its origins; like our neighbors, we considered it a good luck charm.

Because the blood-stained threshold was the family altar, the father led the family in acts of worship at the threshold. First-fruit offerings were often made at the threshold-altar. Incense was burned to the family gods at the threshold-altar. Prayers were offered at the threshold. Marriages were performed at the threshold. If there was evidence of evil spirits or demonic activity, the head of the house would conduct a type of deliverance ritual at the threshold. Anything modern worshipers do at their temples or church houses, ancient people did at the threshold.

It was considered an honor to be buried underneath the threshold as this was close to the household altar and the protecting deity. In Revelation 6:9-10, John tells us that the souls of the believers underneath the altar of God cry out for justice. In Europe and colonial America, ministers and honored saints were buried underneath the altar or pulpit of their churches. Peggy and I have been to the church building in New England where George Whitefield preached. At his death, the people buried him in the basement of the church building right underneath the pulpit. The pastor is also buried there.

The Threshold Blood Covenant and Marriage

I mentioned in Chapter 2 that God considers marriage to be a sacred blood covenant between a man and a woman. It is not a contract—it is a covenant. In Malachi 2:14, God rebuked the husbands for not honoring their marriage covenant. He reminded them, "Yet she is your companion and your wife by covenant."

Ancient people also understood marriage to be a sacred blood covenant relationship. *In view of this, they conducted part of their marriage ceremony at the threshold, and the ceremony always included blood.* While customs differed among people groups and regions, they had some common elements. For example, they all made a blood sacrifice at the threshold of the dwelling where the bride and groom would live.

The threshold was the altar of worship. The sacrifice was for the purpose of establishing a blood covenant with the gods of the house and the new bride and her family. *The bride would not cross the threshold until the covenant sacrifice was made. She would then cross over the bloodstained threshold into the dwelling of her groom.*

They would now be together as husband and wife under the protection and provision of the household gods.

The bridegroom would usually be accompanied by a wedding party of his friends who would celebrate along the way with singing and dancing. The bride may dip her finger in the blood of the animal and smear it on her forehead before crossing the threshold. Or she may prick her finger and put her own blood over the doorpost as a sign of the covenant. Depending on local customs, the bride may kneel and kiss the threshold and give offerings to the household gods before crossing the threshold.

When they consummated the marriage, the virgin bride would shed her own blood in the act of "cutting the covenant of marriage." The friend of the bridegroom was given the bloodstained sheet to show the family as proof that the family was indeed getting a virgin bride as agreed to in the marriage documents. This certainly seems like a most primitive and gross practice to us modern folk. Perhaps this is because we have strayed so far from the biblical understanding of marriage as a blood covenant. Most anything that is truly biblical would seem primitive and strange to us.

Crossing the Threshold

After offering a blood sacrifice to the household gods, the bride would then cross over the threshold and enter the house. She must cross the threshold without stepping on it. If she was veiled, her groom would carry her over the threshold. *We still have this practice today of the groom carrying his bride over the threshold of the room or home where they spend their first night together as husband and wife.*

It was also customary for the guests to pour rice, corn, or seeds on the head of the bridegroom and bride as they crossed the threshold. Sometimes when the bride crossed the threshold, she would toss different kinds of grains, nuts, and small fruits behind her back. *This was an offering to the gods of the household and the covenant of marriage. We still have these "rice tossing" traditions today; we just don't understand their origins and meanings.*

The Threshold Blood Dedication

It was also a common practice to dedicate a new dwelling by offering a blood covenant sacrifice at the threshold. When a new dwelling was built, the owner would not reside in it or cross the threshold until a blood sacrifice was offered at the threshold to the household deity. In the owner's mind, he or she would not be under the protection and provision of the household gods until the sacrifice was offered to the deity. *After the sacrifice was made, the owner would step or leap over the bloodstained threshold and enter the house.*

The covenant with the family deity included all of the family members residing in the house. The owner would then invite the neighbors who stepped across the bloodstained threshold, ate the sacrificed animal with the host, and became part of the covenant with those dwelling in the house. They believed that eating the sacrificed animal was communing with the family deity. He was in them and they were in him. In more recent times, laying a corner stone or foundation stone as a dedication stone for a structure has its roots in a blood-stained threshold dedicated to the household god.

Threshold Blood Covenant Symbols

So far we have learned that the threshold of the doorway was the primitive altar of the household and considered to be sacred.

Because of this understanding, it was natural that people would write or carve various sacred inscriptions on the door. They would also attach different sacred symbols to the door or strike the doorpost with the blood of the sacrifice. Sometimes they would even dip their hand in the blood of the sacrifice and then place their bloodstained hand print on the door. This was all part of a threshold blood covenant.

The inscription they carved or wrote on the door was often the name of their household god. Other times they would write a sacred saying or phrase on the door or door frame. This was their way of dedicating their threshold altar and house to their protecting deity as well as letting everyone know what god they worshiped.

When the One True God called the Hebrews out of Egypt, He used this common primitive custom that they all understood. He told them to write certain words of Scripture (Deuteronomy. 6:4-9; 11:13-21) on the doorposts of their house and on their gates.

God revealed Himself to the people in their culture, so it should not surprise us that He used practices and customs they were familiar with and understood. He renewed and restored the true meaning of practices and customs before they were perverted. He sanctified those that were acceptable to Him while forbidding those that were not.

The Hebrew word for doorpost is *Mezuzah*. The Mezuzah is the container which holds the Scriptures from Deuteronomy which observant Jews, and some Christians, attach to the door of their house. The Hebrew letter *Shin* is written on the outside of the Mezuzah. The Shin stands for "El Shaddai, the Almighty"— the Guardian of the dwellings of Israel and the Jewish people. This is their way of identifying with the God of Israel as their protecting deity.

Over time, the Mezuzah replaced the blood of the lamb on the doorpost of the Jewish home. While for many this is just a Jewish tradition, for others it is a sacred sign on the door to show their worship of the God of Abraham, Isaac, and Jacob. While we are not Jewish, my wife and I have a Mezuzah on our door for the same reason.

Modern folk often attach something to their front door as a way of "making a statement" about who they are and what they believe, what causes are dear to them, who they vote for, etc. You may have something attached to your front door. This modern way of "putting something on the doorpost" dates to ancient times and the threshold covenant.

In the Middle East, Christians are called Notzrim, which means followers of the Man from Nazareth. When the terrorist group ISIS occupies a village in Syria or Iraq, they write the Arabic letter for Notzrim on the door of every house where Christians live. The symbol on the door identifies the occupants as Christians and marks them for death.

The Symbol of the Red Hand of the Covenant

Another common practice connected to the threshold covenant of blood was the symbol of the red hand. As I just mentioned, people would often dip their hand in the blood of the sacrifice and then press their blood-stained hand against the door. Their handprint on the door was the signature of the worshiper expressing his or her devotion through blood covenant to their deity.

As previously explained, in return for their worship and devotion the deity was obligated to provide for and protect the worshiper. *Whenever and wherever the red hand was signed, it represented the covenant relationship between the worshiper and the deity.*

This sign of the red hand was one of the most widespread expressions throughout the ancient world, so much so that it has survived even to our modern times. The example Americans would be most familiar with is the Native American. We have all seen movies showing the Native American Indians riding their horses. What did we often see painted on their horses? A red hand!

The red hand was painted on the horses as a way of expressing their blood covenant with the Great Spirit and calling on him for provision and protection. It was a sign of their threshold blood covenant.

This ancient symbolism of the red hand as an expression of worship eventually evolved into the practice of people lifting up their hands in worship to their god, as we see many times in the Bible. To lift up hands in worship to God is not a charismatic or Pentecostal worship expression; it is an expression of people who know their covenant with God.

The modern custom of lifting our right hand in a courtroom and swearing to tell the truth comes from this ancient rite of the "red hand of covenant." We have so many customs and traditions that are rooted in the threshold blood covenant; we just have lost the understanding of their origins and the sacred meaning they symbolize. As a result, we often say and do things in a shallow way without realizing the covenantal implications of our words and actions.

The Greater Threshold-Crossover Covenant

We have been told that at Passover God passed over or by the dwellings where the blood was applied. But what does this mean? What really happened is so powerful the revelation of it can overwhelm us. Please get this deep down in your spirit. *When the people applied the blood to the threshold and the doorway, they were inviting God to cross over the threshold into their home as their protector from the angel of death.*

God didn't pass over, He crossed over. God entered into a threshold-blood covenant with them. He crossed the bloodstained threshold and stood in the door to keep the executioner from entering the home. Death could not claim them. God Himself was the door. The executioner could only enter the homes of those who did not have blood. Oh my! Did you get that? You may want to read it again and again until the revelation burns in your heart with the fire of God. Lord, may it be so from our mouth to Your ears.

The Threshold Covenant was a picture pointing ancient people to the time when God Himself would make a Threshold Covenant with Himself by Himself for all mankind. The Bible (Galatians 4:4) tell us that in the fullness of time, the One True God, the Creator of heaven and earth, the Great I AM, the One who was, who is, and who is to come crossed over the threshold of time and space and became one of us.

The same God who revealed Himself to the Hebrews in Egypt through the bloodstained threshold would lay aside His blazing glory and dazzling beauty in heaven and become one of us.

Why would God do this? Because God loves us and wants to redeem us from our dreadful fallen condition caused by sin. John 3:16 reads, "For God so loved the world that He gave His only begotten [uniquely born] Son, that whoever believes in Him shall not perish but have everlasting life."

God could not save us from our sins, our sorrows, and the angel of death from His throne in heaven. He had to become one of us; He had to become our near kinsman. This was God's plan from eternity past. The Creator would become the creature. The

Father would become the Son, and in His time the Lord of Glory became a baby in a manger. God would now reveal Himself to the world through the bloodstained tree of His Son.

It should not be hard for us to understand that God could stay on His throne in heaven while at the same time become one of us. A human man can be a father and a son at the same time. The prophet Isaiah spoke of this cosmic exchange of the divine for the human.

Isaiah prophesied that God would cross the threshold of time and space and become one of us. He said, "For unto us a Child is born, unto us a Son is given; and the government will be upon His shoulder. And His name would be called Wonderful, Counselor, Mighty God, Everlasting Father, Prince of Peace" (Isaiah 9:6).

This Holy Child would be the virgin-born Seed of Woman (see Genesis 3:15; Isaiah 7:14). He was virgin born so He would not inherit the nature of sin passed down from the corrupted seed (DNA) of Adam. When He was born, He was recognized as God with us.

Matthew understood His birth as the fulfillment of Isaiah 7:14 and wrote, "'Behold, the virgin shall be with child, and bear a Son, and they shall call His name Immanuel,' which is translated, 'God with us'" (Matthew 1:23). They called His name Jesus (Yeshua in Hebrew), which means salvation. God had come to save us in the person of Jesus of Nazareth.

Our Father in heaven has offered the blood of His own Son at the threshold of the cross (crucifixion tree). This is where the covenant exchange took place. Jesus took our sins into His spirit, our sorrows into His soul, and our sicknesses into His body.

Isaiah spoke of this life-exchange and wrote, "Surely He has borne our griefs and carried our sorrows; yet we esteemed Him stricken, smitten by God, and afflicted. But He was wounded for our transgressions, He was bruised for our iniquities; the chastisement for our peace was upon Him, and by His stripes we are healed. All we like sheep have gone astray; we have turned, every one, to his own way; and the Lord has laid on Him the iniquity of us all" (Isaiah 53:4-6).

Jesus was that carpenter who died on the threshold of the cross. They put His body in a cave. Satan and his followers thought they had conquered the Son of God and foiled God's plan. In their evil ignorance and arrogance, they had no idea they were fulfilling the words of the prophets spoken hundreds of years before. God planned for this and allowed for our salvation. Jesus even said that He would fulfill the sign of Jonah by being dead for three days and three nights (see Matthew 12:40).

Peter explains this was God's eternal plan. He writes of Jesus, "He indeed was foreordained before the foundation of the world, but was manifested in these last days for you who through Him believe in God, who raised Him from the dead and gave Him glory, so that your faith and hope are in God" (1 Peter 1:20-21).

Because Jesus was without sin, God raised Him from the dead and seated Him at the place on honor in heaven. Peter further explains that Jesus, "who has gone into heaven and is at the right hand of God, angels and authorities and powers [demonic spirits] having been made subject to Him" (1 Peter 3:22).

Satan would never cross over the threshold of the cross and accept the covenant sacrifice of Jesus. Therefore, Jesus likens him to a thief who comes to steal, kill, and destroy. While satan has evil intentions toward us, Jesus said that He came to give us life and life more abundantly (see John 10:10). The life that Jesus came to give us is His own glorious, overcoming life living inside us.

Paul writes. "Yet in all these things [righteous suffering] we are more than conquerors through Him who loved us. For I am persuaded that neither death nor life, nor angels nor principalities nor powers, nor things present nor things to come, nor height nor depth, nor any other created thing, shall be able to separate us from the love of God which is in Christ Jesus [Messiah Yeshua] our Lord" (Romans 8:37-39).

When we acknowledge Jesus as our threshold sacrifice, God will enter our house—that is, our lives. His Spirit comes to live inside us. God becomes our protector and provider. *Jesus is the door keeping the evil one from destroying us* (John 10:9). He will defend us from satanic attacks because "He who is in you is greater than he who is in the world" (1 John 4:4) He will meet all our needs and supply our every provision (see Philippians 4:19). He is our covenant God and we are His covenant children.

The hold that satan has on the human race is the fear of death, "Inasmuch then as the children have partaken of flesh and blood, He Himself likewise shared in the same, that through death He might destroy him who had the power of death, that is, the devil, and release those who through fear of death were all their lifetime subject to bondage" (Hebrews 2:14-15).

Jesus has conquered death. Hallelujah! We no longer have to fear it. The blood of Jesus has been applied to the threshold of our life. Paul writes, "But if the Spirit of him who raised Jesus from the dead dwells in you, He who raised Christ [Messiah] from the dead will also give life to your mortal bodies through His Spirit who dwells in you" (Romans 8:11).

John adds these words of encouragement, "Beloved, now we are children of God; and it has not yet been revealed what we shall be, but we know that when He is revealed, we shall be like Him, for we shall see Him as He is" (1 John 3:2).

We have crossed over from being natural people to covenant people—from darkness to light, from sin to righteousness, from bondage to liberty, from defeat to victory, from fear to faith, from sickness to health, from poverty to plenty, from death to life. And at His appointed time, when Jesus returns as the Lion from the Tribe of Judah, He will change our bodies and fashion them like unto His own glorious body, and we shall look upon Him as He is for we shall be like Him.

Let us praise the Lord with King David:

> *Bless the Lord, O my soul; and all that is within me, bless His holy name! Bless the Lord, O my soul, and forget not all His benefits: who forgives all your iniquities, who heals all your diseases, who redeems our life from destruction, who crowns you with lovingkindness and tender mercies, who satisfies your mouth with good things, so that your youth is renewed like the eagle's. ... For as the heavens are high above the earth, so great is His mercy toward those who fear Him; as far as the east is from the west, so far has He removed our transgressions from us* (Psalms 103:1-5, 11-12).

Because of all that God done for us, the writer of Hebrews warns us not to trample under our feet the sacred threshold-blood covenant God has made for us through His Son. He warns us to "step over, not step on" His blood and treat it as if it was a common thing (see Hebrews 10::29).

Dear covenant ones, "Let us hold fast the confession of our hope without wavering, for He who promised is faithful. And let us consider one another in order to stir up love and good works, not forsaking the assembling of ourselves together, and is the manner of some, but exhorting one another, and so much more as you see the Day approaching" (Hebrews 10:23-25). Amen and amen!

Chapter 9

THE SALT COVENANT

Throughout this book I have emphasized the importance of learning as much as we can of the Hebraic culture of the Bible, particularly as it relates to the blood covenant. The reason is, when God gave the revelation of Himself and His Word to the Hebrews, He spoke to them in ways they would understand. He spoke to them in terms of their culture. He used the concepts, customs, and practices they were familiar with to teach them spiritual truths.

Over the years I have had so many people say to me that they wish the Lord would have explained why He did some of the things He did and why He said some of things He said. I have scratched my head and said this many times myself. I imagine you have as well.

Because the people understood their own culture, the Bible does not stop to explain itself to those who already knew their way of life. *Because the culture of the Bible is so different from Western culture, believers who live in the West often struggle to understand the spiritual truths God wants us to learn.* This is particularly true with the biblical understanding of covenants and covenant making, which is the central story of the Bible and the theme of this book.

Now here is just one example. In Matthew 5:13, Jesus says to His followers, "You are the salt of the earth; but if the salt loses its flavor, how shall it be seasoned? It is then good for nothing but to be thrown out and trampled underfoot by men."

When Jesus compared His disciples to salt, He was speaking to them in terms they understood much more clearly than we do today. Their knowledge of the importance and use of salt was a part of their everyday lives. So when He used this phrase, they knew immediately what He meant. So what did Jesus mean when He told them they were the salt of the earth? And how can salt lose its flavor? To understand His statement, we must know something about salt and how people in Bible times viewed salt.

The Importance of Salt

Who would have thought that the subject of salt would be a fascinating subject to study? Salt is mined in various ways from underground salt deposits. I have been to one of the largest salt mine caves in the world in Poland. It is so big elevators are needed to go from one level to the next.

With its severe water shortage, Israel is leading the world in harnessing drinking water from our biggest source of salt—our seas and oceans. California has such a severe water shortage; it is finally requesting help from Israel in learning how to harvest drinking water from the Pacific Ocean.

Salt is not only necessary for life, it is also a remedy for skin diseases such as psoriasis. Europeans flock to the Dead Sea mineral baths to get relief for their itchy skin. There are many uses of salt as an antiseptic, a cleaning agent, for dressing wounds, in preserving and purifying, as a substitute for blood, and thousands of other uses.

China is the largest producer of salt followed by the United States, India, and Germany. These four countries produce about half of the entire world's salt.

According to information provided by salt companies, salt has about 14,000 different uses. Only about 6 percent of salt manufactured goes into food. Another 6 percent goes toward agriculture; 8 percent is used to de-ice highways, 12 percent in purifying water, and a whopping 68 percent in industrial chemicals.

The technical name for salt is sodium chloride because it is about 40 percent sodium and 60 percent chlorine, essential chemicals for life. The human body requires salt because salt regulates the balance of nutrients into the cells of our body. Without this balance, the cells would not be healthy and our bodies would suffer from malnutrition, exhaustion, blood pressure issues, and a host of other physical problems. Our bodies would simply shut down and we would die.

In my study of salt, I have learned that pure, natural sea salt contains more minerals our body needs than any other element on our planet. In additional to sodium and chlorine, sea salt includes water, sulfur, zinc, magnesium, iron, potassium, manganese, copper, calcium, silicon, and numerous other nutrients our bodies must have to be healthy. A famine of salt would devastate a population because we cannot live without salt.

As with many food items needed by our body, companies today buy pure sea salt, extract most of the minerals to be resold to other companies, then put what little is left in a container and sell it to us consumers. This may be one of the reasons people feel "sick and tired," because our bodies are not getting the pure salt they need. While we have plenty of salt, we are "salt poor" because of the quality of the salt we are eating. One of the purest salts is Himalayan.

Throughout history, when governments realized that people required salt to live, they found an easy way to raise money—they taxed the salt. There has been more than one revolution over excessive taxes on salt. America had a "tea revolt" over British taxes on tea, but more revolts have been started over excessive taxes on salt. For example, historians tell us that a major reason for the French Revolution was the excessive tax the French government put on salt.

Governments and companies have sought to monopolize the supply and demand of salt. They did so for financial gain, for competitive advantage in trade, and to control people's lives. Wars have been fought over salt and empires toppled. When Britain ruled India, the British sought to control the population by controlling the supply of salt. Mahatma Gandhi symbolically showed his resistance to British rule by marching to the sea to get his own salt rather than a handout from the British authorities.

Salt has been used as money in trade and as payment for work. People carried salt with them to trade for goods. Ancient cultures used salt as payment for slaves. When the slave was not a good worker, they said he was "not worth his salt." Roman soldiers were often paid with salt. This salt payment was known as "salarium" from which we get the word *salary. Salt is the root word for many English words including the word "salvation."* There is so much more I could share about the history of salt, but let's move on to the subject of the importance and use of salt in Bible times.

In the previous chapter I mentioned H. Clay Trumbull as the author of *The Threshold Covenant.* In his studies of primitive cultures, he also wrote a book entitled, *The Salt Covenant* originally published in 1896. He wrote it for scholars and research historians rather than for a general audience. In 2000, Impact Christian Books republished the book. As in the previous chapter, some of the cultural background and examples I am sharing in this chapter are from his book.

Salt in the Bible

The words *salt, salted,* and *saltness* are found about 44 times in the Bible. Nobody wants to eat bland food, so Bible people seasoned their food with salt just as we do. Job lamented, "Can flavorless food be eaten without salt?" (Job 6:6). But salt had much more importance to people than just seasoning their food.

To ancient people, salt was life and life was salt. It not only flavored their food, it preserved their food and had purifying qualities. Try to imagine living in Bible times when salt was used in everything the people did. People used salt in their sacrificial offerings to their gods. They used salt in healing, in their baths, as a substitute for blood, and as protection against evil spirits. Egyptians used salt to preserve their mummies.

Salt was used as a sign of covenant relationships, as a symbol of honor, friendship, loyalty, hospitality, and in marriage fidelity and commitment. Salt was even used in blessings and curses. It is no wonder that salt was considered to be a sacred commodity.

Salt and Blood

Because the people thought of salt as a sacred commodity, their most important use of salt was in covenant making. Salt was considered an equivalent to blood and was used with blood and as a substitute for blood. *Bible people understood a salt covenant to be like a blood covenant.* As we have learned, a blood covenant was a sacred compact binding people to each other and to their gods in a covenant relationship. Salt was important in covenant making because it added its unique healing, preserving, and purifying qualities.

The human body contains a little over five quarts of blood. There are more than eight teaspoons of salt in our blood. Because blood has salt in it and salt, like blood, was necessary for life, ancient people looked at blood and salt as being almost interchangeable. If blood was not available for sacrifices, salt was used as a substitute. When Henry Stanley went to Africa looking for Dr. Livingston, he reported that the Africans would use salt as a blood substitute.

In modern times, saline injections are given to people who have blood problems. Today in Israel, combat doctors use a saline solution in transfusions on the battlefield until the wounded soldier can be evacuated to a regular medical facility. They have also developed freeze-dried blood packs to assist the wounded.

In the last chapter, we learned about the Threshold Covenant and the blood at the threshold as an expression of covenant making. If a guest came unannounced and there was no time to sacrifice an animal, the host would sprinkle salt on the threshold in place of the blood. People recognized salt as the equivalent or a representative of blood.

The Covenant of Salt in the Sacrificial Offerings

Three times the Bible speaks about a "covenant of salt." Each one connects to Jesus as the blood covenant/salt of the covenant sacrifice greater than bulls and goats, the High Priest greater than Aaron, and the King greater than David. *Wow!* This is truly amazing.

The first mention is in Leviticus where God instructs the priest to put salt in the sacrificial offerings. Leviticus 2:13 reads, "And every offering of your grain offering you shall season with salt; you shall not allow the salt of the covenant of your God to be lacking from your grain offering. With all your offerings you shall offer salt."

Ezekiel further comments about salt in the sacrificial offerings. He says, "When you offer them before the Lord, the priests shall throw salt on them, and they will offer them up as a burnt offering to the Lord" (Ezekiel 43:24).

When ancient pagan people made an offering to their gods, they did so to appease them so the gods wouldn't be angry with the people. But it was not so with the Hebrews. As I have mentioned previously, the Hebrew word for sacrifice is *korban*. It means to come near, to approach, to establish a close relationship with someone. Some people only see a God of wrath in the Old Testament. This is just not true. In God's grace and mercy, He established the sacrifices as a way for the Hebrews to draw near to Him.

Salt represented life, and this is why it was added to the sacrifices. It was God's way of saying that the Hebrews would always have a sacrifice that would preserve them, sanctify them, and flavor their lives with the life and moral character of God. That sacrifice was Jesus of Nazareth.

As we learned in Chapter 5, the sacrificial offerings were a picture of Jesus who gave His life as the ultimate "korban" to God on our behalf. He is our sin offering, our trespass offering, our burnt offering, our meal offering, and our peace offering. Jesus is the once and for all, perfect and everlasting sacrifice.

This is the whole teaching in the book of Hebrews. When the writer of Hebrews says that the New has replaced the Old (see Hebrews 7:22; 8:13), he does not mean that God did away with the Law. Hebrews was written to Jews who were following Jesus. They were confused about making sacrifices at the Temple with the priest as their ancestors had done for centuries.

The writer of the book of Hebrews clarifies this for them and says, "And every priest stands ministering daily and offering repeatedly the same sacrifices, which can never take away sins. But this Man, after he had offered one sacrifice for sins forever, sat down at the right hand of God, from that time waiting till His enemies are made His footstool. For by one offering He has perfected forever those who are being sanctified" (Hebrews 10:11-14).

In context, the writer of the book of Hebrews was simply saying that the sacrifice of Jesus was greater than the sacrifice of animals, that Jesus is a priest greater than Aaron, and that His body was the greater dwelling of God than the Tabernacle of Moses. *So when the writer of Hebrews talks about Jesus replacing the*

Law, he only means the religious or ceremonial aspects of the Law. The true essence of God's Law is to love Him and to love people. That will never change.

We know that salt has elements in it that flavor, purify, and preserve life by retarding the decaying process. This is why companies put loads of salt in processed foods to increase the shelf life of the food. What we get when we buy processed food is a lot of salt and a little food that has had most of its helpful ingredients processed to death. With the help of salt, processed food might taste good but it has very little value. For the sake of your health and that of your children, do your best to buy real food that has not been processed.

We have learned that the animal the people sacrificed to God represented the person making the sacrifice. The animal was dead. *But here is something really, really important for us to know. The addition of the salt was a picture or visual aid of the person presenting himself or herself as a "living" sacrifice to God.* They made the sacrifice with the hope that God would accept it in their place, and in return they desired to live a pure life that would please God and "flavor their community" with His worship and character. While the animal sacrificed was dead, the presence of salt symbolized life for the people.

This understanding is the historical, cultural, Hebraic context and background to Paul's instruction to the Romans. Bible students are very familiar with his statement, "I beseech you, therefore, brethren, by the mercies of God, that you present your bodies a living sacrifice, holy, acceptable to God, which is your reasonable service. And do not be conformed to this world, but be transformed by the renewing of your mind, that you may prove what is that good and acceptable and perfect will of God" (Romans 12:1-2).

The Covenant of Salt in the Priesthood

The second use of the phrase *covenant of salt* is in the book of Numbers. Just as God used salt in the sacrifices as a picture of an everlasting sacrifice, He also used this phrase to speak of an everlasting priesthood.

Numbers 18:19 reads, "All the heave offerings of the holy things, which the children of Israel offer to the Lord, I have given to you and your sons and daughters with you as an ordinance forever; it is a covenant of salt forever before the Lord with you and your descendants with you."

Notice the promise of priesthood is a "covenant of salt." When the Lord called the Hebrews out of Egypt He called them to be a nation of priests to the pagans. Exodus 19:5-6 reads, "Now therefore, if you will indeed obey My voice and keep My covenant, then you shall be a special treasure to Me above all people; for all the earth is Mine. And you shall be to Me a kingdom of priests and a holy nation."

Unfortunately, the people did not obey the Lord. So He chose a special group from the family of Aaron to be His priests for the people. And even though they too failed, God, through the covenant of salt, promised they would always have priestly representation before Him.

Jesus is not only the fulfillment of the everlasting sacrifice; He is also the fulfillment of the everlasting priesthood. While Jesus is not a Levite, His priestly ministry is after the order of Melchizedek, the King of Jerusalem who appeared to Abraham and is called the priest of God Most High (see Genesis 14:18).

Melchizedek was both priest and king. Likewise, Jesus is also priest and king. Because He was resurrected from the dead, His is

240

an everlasting priesthood. Hebrews 7:23-25 says, "Also there were many priests, because they were prevented by death from continuing. But He, because He continues forever, has an unchangeable priesthood. Therefore He is also able to save to the uttermost those who come to God through Him, since He always lives to make intercession for them."

The Covenant of Salt in the Kingdom

The third mention of the covenant of salt is in reference to David's kingdom. In 2 Samuel God made a covenant promise to David that David would always have a descendant who would sit on the throne of Israel.

The promise reads, "When your days are fulfilled and you rest with your fathers, I will set up your seed after you, who will come from your body, and I will establish his kingdom. He shall build a house for My name, and I will establish the throne of his kingdom forever. ...And your house and your kingdom shall be established forever before you. Your throne shall be established forever" (2 Samuel 7:12-13,16).

Wow—what a promise! Later after David and Solomon died, the kingdom was split between North and South. Jeroboam was king of the North and Abijah was king of the South. Abijah was a descendant of King David. In trying to reason with Jeroboam, Abijah reminded him that God made an everlasting covenant of salt with David and his descendants. He said, "Should you not know that the Lord God of Israel gave the dominion over Israel to David forever, to him and his sons, by a covenant of salt?" (2 Chronicles 13:5).

In this instance, Abijah appeals to Jeroboam on the basis of the sacred covenant of salt. The idea is that God's promise to

David was forever and that Jeroboam should put down his weapons and not attack Abijah. As the story unfolds, the Lord gave Abijah a great victory. We read in 2 Chronicles 13:18, "the children of Judah prevailed, because they relied on the Lord God of their fathers."

The New Testament proclaims that Jesus is that greater Son of David. When Jesus was born, Luke applies the prophecy given to King David to Jesus. He says these words about Jesus, "He will be great, and will be called the Son of the Highest; and the Lord God will give Him the throne of His father David. And He will reign over the house of Jacob forever, and of His kingdom there will be no end" (Luke 1:32-33). Whenever people called Jesus the Son of David, they were acknowledging Him as the Messiah.

In the book of Revelation, Jesus is called the "Lion from the Tribe of Judah" and the "Root and Offspring of David" (see Revelation 5:5; 22:16). By the blood of the everlasting covenant seasoned with salt, Jesus is the greater Son of David. He is not only King of Israel but King of Kings and Lord of Lords.

Using Salt Against Evil Spirits

One of the characteristics of salt is that when we rub it on our skin, it is absorbed into our body. Because of its purifying and preserving nature, Bible people and those living in the Middle East would rub salt on newborn babies. They believed that doing so would give the baby good health and protect him or her against evil. This was such a powerful custom; some people still do this today.

We see a reference to this in the Bible. When God reminded the Hebrews of their pitiful condition when He called them to be His own people, He said, "As for your nativity, on the day you were born your navel cord was not cut, nor were you washed in water to cleanse you; you were not rubbed with salt nor wrapped in swaddling clothes" (Ezekiel 16:4).

In many ways, Middle Eastern culture today is still close to the culture of the Bible. Those who know their ancient customs believe if a child grows up to be sickly, it is because "the child was not salted when he or she was born." It was common for Arab parents to protect their children by placing salt in their hands as the women sprinkled salt in the house while rebuking evil spirits.

Here are some more customs that tell us how people thought of salt. Women would wash themselves with salt after giving birth to protect themselves against evil spirits. Sometimes parents would place a small bag of salt in the baby's clothing to protect the baby from evil spirits.

Salt was also used as a protection against witches. For example, if a witch assaulted a person, the person believed he or she could bring about the witch's death by forcing the witch to give him or her bread with salt. People who committed murder would eat bread with salt immediately after their crime. They believed that by doing this they could prevent the return of their victim's spirit to revenge his death. When people moved into a new house they would bring bread with salt into the house in order to protect the house against evil spirits. This is the origin of the modern custom of people throwing salt over their shoulders for good luck.

Salt as a Blessing and a Curse

Salt was considered a blessing to the righteous but a curse to the unrighteous. We see this in a story about the prophet Elisha. When Elisha began his ministry, the people at Jericho had bad water. They begged Elisha to heal or cleanse their spring so they could have good water to drink and for their land.

Here's the story recorded in 2 Kings 2:19-22:

Then the men of the city said to Elisha, "Please notice, the situation of this city is pleasant, as my lord sees; but the water is bad, and the ground barren." And he [Elisha] said, "Bring me a new bowl, and put salt in it." So they brought it to him. Then he went out to the source of the water, and cast in the salt there, and said, "Thus says the Lord: 'I have healed this water; from it there shall be no more death or barrenness.'" So the water remains healed to this day, according to the word of Elisha which he spoke.

People in Bible times believed that a salt spring was a gift from their gods. They considered themselves to be righteous in the eyes of their gods and the salt spring was their proof. But a spring without salt was considered a curse from their gods. This was also true of their land. Any farmer, or anyone with weeds in their yard, can tell you that if you sow salt on the land, it kills the weeds and the soil. An application of salt can turn a productive land into barren land that won't produce. *In the Bible, a land that has been salted is considered a judgment against the wicked. Both ancient and modern Israel is a clear witness to this fact.*

When Moses gave his last sermon to the people, he warned them that if they broke the covenant with their God, they would not have His blessings on the land. The Promised Land flowing with milk and honey would be barren. The land would be cursed. People would look at the land and wonder in unbelief how it could be so barren and uninhabitable. Moses explains:

So that the coming generation of your children who rise up after you, and the foreigner who comes from a far land, would say, when they see the plagues of that land and the sicknesses which the Lord has laid on it: "The whole land is brimstone, salt and burning; it is not sown, nor does it bear, nor does any grass grow there..." All nations would say, "Why has the Lord done so to this land? What does the heat of this great anger mean?" Then people would say: "Because they have forsaken the covenant of the Lord God of their fathers, which He made with them when He brought them out of the land of Egypt" (Deuteronomy 29:22-25). (see also Leviticus 26.)

If you know the history of the land you know this is exactly what happened. Because the Hebrews forsook God and His covenant, the land was cursed. It was uninhabitable and nothing would grow there. This is why no empire ever gave any thought to the land. This is why no people group, such as the mythical Palestinians, ever made it an independent state or nation or ever established a capital in the land, other than the Jewish people. They took one look at the land and said, "Forget it—nothing could ever grow here." *Even though the land was salted (cursed), God used this to keep the land safe for the time when He would bring His ancient people back to Israel and once again bless the land.*

When Mark Twain visited the land in 1867 he wrote it was a land that sat in sackcloth and ashes, desolate and unlovely. Mark Twain considered the land to be the most God-forsaken place he had ever seen. It was cursed with the salt of the covenant.

However, if you have been to Israel you know that God has "unsalted the land." The desert is blossoming like a rose as God said it would in Isaiah 35:1. Israel is a miracle. Not only because the people are back but so is the land. Modern Israel is a beautiful country with flowers and produce growing in places you would never imagine. Israel raises fish in the desert and ships Easter lilies to Holland that are then shipped around the world. Every day, Israel trucks food to Jordan and Gaza feeding the very enemies who want to destroy her. If you have ever been on a tour to Israel, you know exactly what I am talking about.

Another example of the curse of salt on the land of the wicked is in the book of Judges. Here is what happened. When Abimelech defeated the men of Shechem, he destroyed the city and surrounding area by sowing it with salt. We read, "So Abimelech fought against the city all that day; he took the city and killed the people who were in it; and he demolished the city and sowed it with salt" (Judges 9:45).

The prophet Jeremiah connected a barren heart with barren land. He writes, "Thus says the Lord, 'Cursed is the man who trusts in man and makes flesh his strength, whose heart departs from the Lord. For he shall be like a shrub in the desert, and shall not see when good comes, but shall inherit the parched places in the wilderness, in a salt land which is not inhabited" (Jeremiah 17:5-6). In the next verses, 7-8, Jeremiah says the man who trusts in the Lord will be blessed with a fruitful land.

The prophet Ezekiel also mentions the difference between salted and unsalted land. He makes his point that the river flowing from the Temple during the Millennium will be a river of healing but that "its swamps and marshes will not be healed; they will be given over to salt" (Ezekiel 47:11).

Salt as a Covenant Bond of Friendship and Loyalty

Because of the preserving nature of salt, it was used like blood as a symbol of an enduring covenant. Like a blood covenant, a salt covenant was considered a sacred bond between people. Whenever people ate salt with someone, they entered into a covenant relationship with them. If you ate salt with someone, you were responsible for their protection as well as their provisions. They came under your care. On the contrary, it would be the highest dishonor to harm someone with whom you ate salt.

The normal way people ate salt with someone was by sharing a meal. Bread was part of every meal, so salt was added to the bread. Therefore, to eat bread with someone was the same as to "eat salt" with them. If a person ate salt with someone but then tried to harm them, it was said that "Their bread had no salt in it." Another way of saying the same thing was that "salt was not in their stomachs." Other sayings for someone who did not honor the salt covenant were that the person was "one untrue to salt" or that they were "salt abusers."

If a person ate salt with someone and then betrayed them it was said that they "betrayed the salt." If they tried to hurt them through physical harm or theft of their goods or any violation of their family honor, the person would be violating the most sacred of customs. He would bring shame to his family and be considered an outcast.

There are many fascinating stories in Middle Eastern Arab culture that illustrate this custom, which was their way of life. One you may be familiar with is the tale of "Ali Baba and the Forty Thieves." Many of us grew up reading this story, but we may not have fully understood the significance of the story.

According to the story, a leader of a band of robbers visited Ali Baba in order to murder him. He disguised himself so Ali Baba would not recognize him. When it came time to eat the meal, the evil man refused to eat food that had salt in it. Ali Baba's slave girl noticed this and wondered, "Who is he that eats only meat that has no salt in it?" She then realized it was the robber and said to herself, "So this is the reason why the villain does not eat salt. He came here to slay my master who is his mortal enemy." As evil as this man was, he was not willing to "eat salt" with the man he was going to murder. He would not violate the covenant of salt.

Older Middle Eastern Arab people still have an understanding of what it means to eat salt with someone. Peggy and I have our own story. Years ago, we visited the home of an Arab friend who lives in an Arab village near Jerusalem. The neighborhood was not a "Western-Christian-friendly" place.

In spite of us being "foreigners," Arabs are known for their hospitality. We did not have long to visit so we went in the afternoon when we thought they would not prepare a meal for us. *But as soon as we got there, the father of our friend greeted us with these words, "I want to eat salt with you."* Yes, he really said that, and thank God we knew what that meant.

He said he wanted to have a meal with us. He said we were welcome into his home. He said because we knew his son, we were his honored guests. He said we were under his protection as long as we were in the neighborhood. He said whatever he had that we needed he would be glad to give us.

We have never had a Christian make this kind of commitment to us even though we have been in the ministry for over 40 years. It is because those of us who live in the West do not have a biblical culture. We don't understand some of the most basic fundamentals of our relationship to God and to one another because the relationship is based on a sacred blood-threshold-salt covenant.

We were amazed by his words. We are Western Christians. I am a minister of Jesus. And this man was a Muslim who had never even met us. He had Islamic decorations in his home. He had wall rugs of the Dome of the Rock. He had the Koran on his table and sayings of Mohammed. His religion represented everything that we oppose. But his culture was right out of the Bible.

We enjoyed a wonderful time of food, fellowship, and friendship and then went our way. Later we realized a powerful truth. *We were the honored guest of the father because we knew the son. Wow!*

The Table as an Altar

In biblical times, people viewed their table at home where they had their meals as a family altar. The bread, seasoned with salt, and the wine at the table represented the sacrificial offering and the blood covenant relationship between the family members with their god and with each other.

The meal and table fellowship meant much more to the people than just a place to eat. It was that but it was more than that. It was also considered a sacred part of their home worship experience. *Because of this view, the people did not bless the food. They blessed the Lord, or their gods, for their food.* Any food that fell from the table was not to be picked up and eaten because, in the people's minds, it had fallen from the altar.

This is the background and understanding of the story in Matthew 15:21-28. Bible students know this story well. It is the story of the Gentile woman who came to Jesus begging Him to heal her daughter. Because Jesus was called to His own Jewish people, He did not respond to her and His disciples wanted Him to send her away. Jesus said to her:

> *"It is not good to take the children's bread and throw it to the little dogs." But she persisted and responded, "Yes,*

Lord, but even the little dogs eat the crumbs which fall from their masters' table." Then Jesus answered and said to her, "O woman, great is your faith! Let it be to you as you desire." And her daughter was healed from that very hour (Matthew 15:26-28).

To the Western mind, Jesus seemed unkind to the woman. But He was simply acting within the culture of His times and His people.

Later, when the Temple was destroyed and the people scattered, their table where they had their meals replaced the sacrifices and became their family altar. Today, when observant Jews have their Shabbat meals, they give the blessing over the bread and then sprinkle salt on the bread before breaking it and passing it to the family members. This is a memorial to the "salt covenant."

The great Jewish sage, Abraham Joshua Heschel, said, "Every home should be a temple, every table an altar, and all of life a song to God." May we as the covenant people of God live with such an understanding and practice in our everyday lives.

You Are the Salt of the Earth

Now that we have this background of how Bible people understood salt, I think we can understand what Jesus meant when He called His disciples the salt of the earth. I pointed out that the phrase *covenant of salt* is used three times. It is used specifically in reference to sacrifices, priesthood, and kingship.

These three references to the salt covenant point us to Jesus as the One who perfectly lived out the sacred covenant of salt with His Father in heaven. Jesus said, "I always do those things that please Him [the Father]" (John 8:29). Therefore He is the ultimate sacrifice for our sins. He is our great High Priest who ever lives to make intercession for us. He is the greater Son of David who is King of Kings and Lord of Lords. His life and His example season humanity with the moral flavor of the character of God that preserves and purifies our lives and keeps us from corrupting ourselves.

How can Jesus "salt humanity" when He is not now living among us? He is physically in heaven. It is a certainty that He will return at His appointed time. But until then, the world can't see Him or hear Him. Jesus desires a company of people to be His human body on the earth. He wants a people He can live His life through—a people who will salt the earth with His moral life and teachings. He is calling a people who will enter into a sacred blood-threshold-salt covenant with Him. Dear reader, precious and beloved of God, we are these people.

Jesus said it this way, "And I will pray the Father, and He will give you another Helper [Comforter], that He may abide with you forever—the Spirit of truth, whom the world cannot receive, because it neither sees Him nor knows Him; but you know Him for He dwells with you and will be in you" (John 14:16-17).

God's plan is to reveal Himself on earth through His people. Being a believer is so much more than just saying a prayer of salvation and then going to heaven when we die. We are to manifest heaven on earth by the way we live. We are to follow Jesus, learn of Jesus, imitate Jesus, and reproduce His life into the lives of others. The Spirit of God does this work in us, through us, and out of us.

Remember that salt is the root word for the English word *salvation*. Jesus, Yeshua in Hebrew, means salvation. *As the salt of the earth, believers are "carriers" of salvation.* We carry the life of the Savior in us. As carriers of salvation, we give our lives as a living sacrifice. We die to ourselves (the sacrifice) but live for God (the salt).

As carriers of God's salvation, we are God's priestly representatives on the earth. Peter explains, "But you are a chosen generation, a royal priesthood, a holy nation, His own special people, that you may proclaim the praises of Him who called you out of darkness into His marvelous light" (1 Peter 2:9). When we live out our high calling as God's priests on the earth, we preserve, purify, and flavor those around us with the life of God's Spirit living in us and ministering through us.

As carriers of God's salvation, we live under His righteous rule. He is not just our Savior; He is our Lord and King. We embrace Jesus as Lord and invite the Holy Spirit to rule over our soul. The spiritual nature of His Kingdom flows out of our soul into our bodies and is manifested to the world in the way we live. The Kingdom of God in us ministers the life-giving, preserving, purifying flavor of God's rule into the lives of our family, our community, our nation, and our world.

How should we live as followers of Jesus? What should the world see when they look at us? While we are not perfect, they should see our blood-threshold-salt covenant Savior and Lord living His life in us. They should see Jesus who promises to protect us from our enemies and provide for our every need. His Spirit in us is greater than the spirit of the world (see 1 John 4:4). His provision is all that we need to serve Him (see Philippians 4:19). His strength in us enables us to do the supernatural (see Philippians 4:13).

God's love in us is greater than hate. His forgiveness in us is greater than revenge. His liberty in us is greater than legalism.

His mercy in us is greater than judgmentalism. His peace in us is greater than worry. His faith in us is greater than fear. His hope in us is greater than despair. His truth in us is greater than lies. His blessing in us is greater than curses. His concern in us for others is greater than selfishness. His servant heart in us is greater than self-serving. His generosity in us is greater than stinginess. His goodness in us is greater than evil. His compassion in us is greater than indifference. His justice in us is greater than wrongdoing.

His supply in us is greater than need. His joy in us is greater than sorrow. His beauty in us is greater than ugliness. His wisdom in us is great than confusion. His gentleness in us is greater than harshness. His kindness in us is greater than meanness. His purity in us is greater than lust. His righteousness in us is greater than sin. His greatness in us is greater than failure. His healing in us is greater than sickness. His victory in us is greater than defeat. His light in us is greater than darkness. His life in us is greater than death.

This is what Jesus meant when He said we are the salt of the earth. Natural salt makes people thirsty. *As we "salt the world" through the way we live, our holy lives makes people thirsty for what we have.* They want what we have, and what we have is a Person. Jesus invites all of us to come to the Father through Him. We can be the honored guest of the Father because we know the Son. Jesus said, "If anyone serves Me, him My Father will honor" (John 12:26).

Chemists explain that salt cannot lose it flavor. So what did Jesus mean when His said if salt loses its flavor it is good for nothing? While salt cannot lose its chemical makeup, it can lose its effectiveness to flavor, preserve, and purify. How does this happen? *Salt can lose its effectiveness if it has been mixed with too much of other compounds.* It is still salt, but it is no longer effective. We have all experienced this with our food. If we do not have enough salt on our food, we add more for the flavor. The salt is there; we just cannot taste it.

Likewise, we can lose our effectiveness by compromising our values, our convictions, our priorities, and our way of life with the world. As God's people, we are still the salt of the earth, but nobody can "taste and see that the Lord is good." We are not making people thirsty for the Lord. This is why God's holy Word warns us not to embrace a worldly lifestyle. John writes:

> *Do not love the world or the things in the world. If anyone loves the world, the love of the Father is not in him. For all that is in the world—the lust of the flesh, the lust of the eyes, and the pride of life—is not of the Father but is of the world. And the world is passing away, and the lust of it; but he who does the will of God abides forever* (1 John 2:15-17).

When believers live worldly, we "betray the salt." We betray our Lord and lose our saltiness. Because we have "eaten salt" with our Lord, we present ourselves as a living sacrifice to God. While protecting ourselves and loved ones against evil, we love our enemies and bless those who curse us. We do good to those who hate us and who spitefully use us and persecute us. We minister as His priests on the earth bringing wholeness to those around us. We live as Kingdom people under the rule of Jesus. We seek first His Kingdom knowing that all these other things will be added unto us. We extend His Kingdom life to those around us. We speak the truth in love. Our word is our bond and testimony of the faithfulness of our God.

We do not have this salt life within ourselves. We have it in Him and He lives in us. We impart His life in us to others. We preserve spiritual life and hinder the decay of spiritual death. We purify the spiritual conditions around us. We honor God by honoring our word. Our holy lives in Him make people thirsty for righteousness. We flavor the world with our godly lives. We are the salt of the earth.

Leonardo da Vinci and the Last Supper

I want to close with a comment on the greatest of all Christian paintings. It is Leonardo da Vinci's painting of the Last Supper. I never paid much attention to it until I wrote this chapter.

In 1495, Leonardo was commissioned to paint a wall in the dining hall of the Santa Maria delle Grazie church complex in Milan, Italy. He was asked to paint Jesus with His disciples at what became known as "The Last Supper." Of course, this was the Passover meal Jesus celebrated with His disciples. This last supper Passover meal evolved into the communion or covenant meal for believers. Da Vinci worked on the painting for three years before completing it in 1498. He painted the Last Supper as if it was a meal eaten by the people of his time. By doing so, it is technically wrong in every detail.

For example, the painting shows Jesus and the disciples eating when the sun is out when we all know the Passover meal was at night. The shape of the table is incorrect because Jesus and the disciples ate at a horseshoe shaped table called a "triclinium." Da Vinci wanted to paint the disciples in a certain way, so he also took liberty with the location in which they are seated. In the Bible, John was seated to the right of Jesus and Judas to His left in the place of honor. In this painting both John and Judas are seated to the right of Jesus.

However, this is not the point. The brilliance of the painting is that da Vinci wanted to paint the Last Supper in a way to show how the disciples reacted when Jesus told them that one of them would betray Him (see John 13:21-30). When Jesus said this, the Bible says, "Then the disciples looked at one another, perplexed about whom He spoke" (John 13:22).

I encourage you to look at pictures of the painting on the Internet. You will notice the different reactions and expressions on the faces of the disciples. It is truly a brilliant painting. Who is the one who will betray the Lord? Who is the one who will "betray the salt"?

Da Vinci gives us a clue. What is this clue da Vinci has given us? What did he paint for only those who have eyes to see? As you look at the painting, Judas is the third one to the left of Jesus— His right if you were sitting with Him. You can further identify Judas because he is holding the money bag. However, there is something else about Judas that is much more important and revealing. If you look closely with a full screen of the painting, you will notice something on the table in front of Judas by his arm. It is a cup of spilt salt. Judas is the one who ate salt with our Lord but betrayed Him. He is the one who "betrayed the salt."

May it not be said of us that we "betrayed the salt" by the way we live. Instead, may we salt the earth with the life of Jesus.

REVIEW STUDY QUESTIONS

Chapter 1: Introduction to a Dusty Old Book

1. Explain the phrase, "The Hebrew Bible is a picture of a person."

2. Explain how Jesus said the Hebrew Bible and the New Testament are linked to tell one story.

3. Try to memorize how Jesus is pictured in every book of the Bible. It would be fun to find a study partner and memorize it together.

_____

_____

_____

_____

_____

_____

Chapter 2: The Blood Covenant

1. Explain the meaning of the word "covenant."

_____

_____

_____

_____

_____

_____

_____

_____

2. Briefly describe the covenant exchange that took place at the cross.

_____

_____

_____

_____

_____

_____

_____

3. Explain how you can apply this knowledge to your life and what this means to you personally.

_____

_____

_____

_____

_____

_____

_____

Chapter 3: What Did Abraham Believe?

1. Explain why Abraham was able to have faith in God's promises and how you can do the same.

---

2. Briefly describe how God preached the gospel to Abraham and how this is a picture of Jesus.

---

3. Explain how you an apply this knowledge to your life and what this means to you personally.

Chapter 4: The Tabernacle

1. Explain why God gave the Ten Commandments and what this means to you personally.

2. Explain the purpose of the Tabernacle and how the furnishings pictured Jesus.

3. Explain how you can apply this knowledge to your life what this means to you personally.

_____

_____

_____

_____

Chapter 5: The Sacrifices

1. List the five types of sacrificial offerings and the purpose of each.

_____

_____

_____

_____

_____

2. Explain why God established the sacrificial offering and how each is a picture of Jesus.

_____

_____

_____

_____

_____

_____

3. Explain how you can apply this knowledge to your life what this means to you personally.

_____

_____

_____

_____

_____

_____

Chapter 6: The High Priest

1. Explain why God established the priesthood and how it is a picture of Jesus.

_____

_____

_____

_____

_____

_____

2. Describe the work of the High Priest on the Day of Atonement.

_____

_____

_____

_____

_____

_____

3. Explain how you can apply this knowledge to your life and what this means to you personally.

_____

_____

_____

_____

_____

Chapter 7: The Passover

1. Explain the purpose and practice of Passover.

_____

_____

_____

_____

_____

2. Explain how Passover is a picture of Jesus.

_____

_____

_____

_____

_____

_____

3. Explain how you can apply this knowledge to your life and what this means to you personally.

_____

_____

_____

_____

_____

_____

Chapter 8: The Threshold Covenant

1. Explain the purpose and practice of the Threshold Covenant.

_____

_____

_____

_____

_____

2. Explain how the Threshold Covenant is a picture of Jesus.

_____

_____

_____

_____

_____

_____

3. Explain how you can apply this knowledge to our life and what this means to you personally.

_____

_____

_____

_____

_____

Chapter 9: The Salt Covenant

1. Explain the purpose and practice of the Salt Covenant.

_____

_____

_____

_____

_____

2. Explain how the Salt Covenant is a picture of Jesus.

_____

_____

_____

_____

_____

_____

3. Explain how you can apply this knowledge to your life and what this means to you personally.

_____

_____

_____

_____

_____

ABOUT THE AUTHOR

Richard Booker, MBA, PhD., is an ordained Christian minister, President of Sounds of the Trumpet, Inc., and the Founder/Director of the Institute for Hebraic-Christian Studies. Prior to entering the ministry, Dr. Booker had a successful business career. He is the author of more than 40 books, which are used by churches and Bible schools around the world. They have been translated into numerous languages with approximately 500,000 copies in print. He has also developed numerous seminars on practical Christianity.

Dr. Booker has traveled extensively for 40 years teaching in churches and at conferences on various aspects of the Christian life as well as Israel and the Hebraic roots of Christianity. He and his wife, Peggy, have led yearly tour groups to Israel where, for 18 years, he was a speaker at the International Christian Celebration of the Feast of Tabernacles in Jerusalem. This gathering is attended by 5,000 Christians from 100 nations.

Dr. Booker's teachings are designed to help believers better understand the Bible and their covenant God, while sharing biblical truths on how to live an abundant Christian life. His seminars and books are unique in that they contain the meat of the Scriptures in a clear, easy-to-understand language with practical application for everyday Christian living. He has a God-given ability to communicate the Scriptures with a freshness and clarity that brings life out of the Bible and into people's hearts. They enlighten, inspire, and challenge believers in a positive way to live as salt and light.

Dr. Booker and his wife co-founded the Institute for Hebraic-Christian Studies (IHCS) in 1997 as a ministry to educate Christians in the Hebraic culture and background of the Bible, build relationships between Christians and Jews, and give comfort and support to the people of Israel. Through this ministry, they conducted a monthly celebration event in Houston, a formal school on the Biblical Hebraic roots of Christianity and have worked with the Jewish community and the government of Israel to stand against anti-Semitism and give comfort and support to the people of Israel. Their tireless work on behalf of Christians and Jews has been recognized around the world as well as being represented at the Knesset Christian Allies Caucus.

Dr. Booker has available a complete curriculum on the Hebraic roots and culture of the Bible and Christianity. There are 6 core courses and numerous elective courses. Those who take the core courses for credit may earn a Diploma in Hebraic-Christian Studies. You may take the courses online or we can ship the physical product to you. See his web site for details.

Additionally, Dr. Booker has made almost 600 television programs that can be seen on the Internet at www.godslearningchannel.com or via satellite. He also authored hundreds of articles and has produced study material on the biblical Hebraic roots of Christianity for small group study, families, and homeschoolers. He is a spiritual father to many believers around the world.

If you would like to know more about the author, order his study materials, or invite him to speak to your congregation or conference, please contact him at 936-441-2171 or see his Website and online bookstore at www.soundsofthetrumpet.com or www.rbooker.com.

THE MIRACLE OF THE SCARLET THREAD
Study Guide
For Individual and Group Study

This is an easy-to-use interactive study guide to assist you in your own deeper and more personal self-discovery of this life changing subject.

In a convenient 8½ by 11 format, the guide is organized with space for you to write your own insights and personalize and internalize your Spirit-inspired thoughts.

There is a lesson for each chapter of the book. Each lesson reviews the purpose of the chapter, a study outline, a place for personal reflection, a Scripture meditation and a summary and application.

The study guide is perfect for individual or group study as it provides opportunity for input from all members of the study group. It also makes a great teaching tool.

You can order the study guide
from our web store at
www.rbooker.com